Realism
an essay in interpretation
and social reality

REALISM

an essay in interpretation
and social reality

by DAVID J. LEVY

Carcanet New Press, Manchester

In memory of George Levy
1899-1975

Levy, D.
  Realism.
  1. Realism in literature
  I. Title
  809'.912   PN56.R3

First published in Great Britain in 1981
by Carcanet New Press
330 Corn Exchange Buildings
Manchester M4 3BG

© 1981 David J. Levy
SBN 85635 3000

The publisher acknowledges the financial assistance
of the Arts Council of Great Britain

Printed in Great Britain by Billings
London, Guildford and Worcester

Contents

Acknowledgments

I am grateful to the Editor and publishers of *Modern Age* for allowing me to draw on material published in their pages for much of chapter seven; and to the Editor and publishers of *Philosophy Today* for permission to republish the substance of my paper 'Marcuse, Metaphysics and Marxism' in chapter six.

I thank the following for permission to include quotations: University of Notre Dame Press for those from *Anamnesis* by Eric Voegelin; Martinus Nijhoff for those from Alfred Schutz *Collected Papers* and for those from Eric Voegelin 'The Eclipse of Reality' in *Phenomenology and Social Reality* edited by Maurice Natanson; Penguin Books Ltd for those from Herbert Marcuse *Negations,* reprinted by permission of Penguin Books Ltd; and Routledge & Kegan Paul Ltd for quotations from Theodore W. Adorno, *Negative Dialectics.*

Nor would my acknowledgments be complete without thanking Kathleen Gallimore and Pam Atkinson for their help in preparing my manuscript.

1 What is Social Reality?

Modern sociology began as an attempt to found an objective science of society. It was not the first such attempt: the classical political philosophy of Plato and Aristotle and the work of Jean Bodin and of Thomas Hobbes in the seventeenth century were motivated by a similar ambition and the spur to each of them can be found in the circumstances of the time. Reference to the historical background or the social roots of a theory tells us nothing about the truth or validity of that theory; questions of truth are philosophical and not social-scientific. But the history and sociology of knowledge can cast considerable light on the circumstances in which a particular type of intellectual endeavour is likely to be attempted. It is enough to say that the attempt to found an objective science of society is made only at a time of exceptional insecurity, when the day-to-day order of social life is or seems to be threatened with disintegration. The fratricidal chaos that marked the approaching fall of the order of the Greek city state impelled the work of Plato and Aristotle. The break-up of Christendom and the religiously motivated civil strife of post-Reformation Europe gave rise to the work of Hobbes and Bodin. The shock waves of the French Revolution, in combination with the transforming power of industrialization (visible in advance from corners of Europe to which the English factory system had not yet penetrated), created the circumstances in which Saint-Simon, Comte and their contemporaries set out to build the positive science of society to which they gave the name of sociology.

These three attempts to achieve an objective science of society differ from each other in various ways, but all can be understood as attempts to found social order in a realm of objective reality untouched by mere opinion, preference, or prejudice. Each is a reaction against the threat of chaos, for it is only at times of considerable security that sane men scoff at the notions of law and order. And each tries to establish roots in a level of truth that could, in principle, command assent from every rational being. The paradigm for all such attempts is Aristotle's claim to set *episteme politike*, objective insight into the nature of political society based upon knowledge of the nature of man, against mere opinion or *doxa*. Bodin and Hobbes appealed to the need for security, clear to those living through the horrors of civil war, while positivist social science founded its claim to truth in the application to social reality of a natural scientific method

1

which, in a world of religious doubt and political dispute, seemed able to guarantee assent. If we apply the methods of the natural sciences to the study of society, Comte and his successors believed, then the findings of sociology will carry the same weight as the findings of physics. The social order will be as little a subject for dispute as the natural order.

This positivist programme has many virtues, though not virtues likely to commend it to its more radical critics. By emphasizing the importance of careful study and direct observation in social science, its determination to see men as they are and not as it might wish them to be, it guards us against the wish-fulfilling fantasy that is sometimes substituted for sociology. By stressing the discovery of natural laws of social life it draws our attention to the constants that exist between societies of different types in other times and places. Yet the positivist approach is a limiting one which, *at* the limit, falsifies the understanding of social reality which it tries to achieve.

What is the positivist view of science? The practice of science, says the positivist, consists in the discovery of predictive natural laws. In every area of reality the observer will discover a number of regular connections between separate facts. For example, when water is heated at a certain atmospheric pressure to a certain temperature it is vapourized as steam. The correct formulation of a natural law will depend upon accurate observation, and the explanation of any particular fact will consist in its being subsumed under an already formulated law. Scientific laws are statements of regularities between observed items of data. In principle such statements can be expressed mathematically because even where there is no one-for-one correspondence between a particular fact and the relevant law the relationship is a statistical likelihood. We cannot mathematically determine the chances of a particular widow taking her own life, but we can, says Durkheim in his study *Suicide* (a classic of positivist social science) determine on the basis of statistical records the degree to which widows as a class are more likely to take their own lives than women whose spouses are still living.

From the methodological standpoint the positivist does not distinguish between the realm of the natural and the social sciences. In both he sees a world of facts open to observation, that may be charted and understood. The object in sociology is to apply the methods already proved in the natural sciences to society. Only when this is done can we claim to have a 'scientific' understanding of society, for the positivist criterion of science is a methodological one and the methods in question are those of the mathematizing natural sciences and physics in particular. One problem with this is the unexamined assumption that the areas of natural and social science are sufficiently similar to justify the use of the same type of investigatory methods. Later, I shall argue that there is a necessary connection between natural and social reality, that each real society is a particular human solution to a number of natural and cognitive needs traceable to the nature of man and his place in the universe, but this is not in itself sufficient warrant for the positivist programme. There is no one model of 'science' applicable to all reality, for there is no one type of object that the various branches of knowledge study. The criterion for scientific status is not conformity to a model but adequacy of range and method to the object studied. The range and method of the inquirer should be rationally defensible and the grounds for his procedures should be publicly available. Insight, hunches and intuition are not the stuff of science but scientific discoveries and theories flow from them, and the level of science is achieved when the procedures of the scientist are, in principle, available to others. He must not show conformity to any model of 'correct' procedure but logical consistency and revelatory force. This claim is not original but even among those who nod agreement there will be few who see at once the full significance of what it must mean for the sciences of man. I aim to explore this significance in the pages that follow.

Eric Voegelin has pointed out that two fundamental assumptions underlie the positivist programme. First, the success of the natural sciences gave rise to the belief

> that the methods used in the mathematizing sciences of the external world were possessed of some inherent virtue and that all other sciences would achieve comparable success if they followed the example and accepted these methods as their model. This belief by itself was a harmless idiosyncrasy that would have died out when the enthusiastic admirers of the model method set to work in their own sciences and did not achieve the expected successes. It became dangerous because it combined with the second assumption that the methods of the natural sciences were a criterion for theoretical relevance in general.[1]

This second assumption reverses the proper relationship between method and scientific relevance:

> Science is a search for truth concerning the nature of the various realms of being. Relevant in science is whatever contributes to the success of the search. Facts are relevant in so far as their knowledge contributes to the study of essence, while methods are adequate in so far as they can be effectively used as a means for this end. Different objects require different methods. A political scientist who tries to understand the meaning of Plato's *Republic* will not have much use for mathematics; a biologist who studies a cell structure will not have much use for methods of classical philology and principles of hermeneutics. . . . If the adequacy of a method is not measured by its usefulness to the purpose of science, if on the contrary the use of a method is made the criterion of science, then the meaning of science as a truthful account of the structure of reality, as the theoretical orienta-

tion of man in his world, and as the great instrument for man's understanding of his own position in the universe is lost.[2]

The question of methodological adequacy cannot be answered a priori. Only the results of an investigation and the light these results may throw on our initial problem will tell us whether or not we have followed a worthwhile path.

᛫ Voegelin contrasts the methods appropriate to the study of cell structure and those suitable to the understanding of Plato's *Republic*. Why should the methods of the mathematizing natural sciences be suitable to the study of the former and not of the latter? In both cases the scientist is in the presence of data that exist in the external natural world. In both he wishes to understand those data. Both the biological cell and Plato's book can be shown to possess an inherent structure, and an adequate understanding of each involves proper identification of structure. Nevertheless the structures in question exist on different levels. In the case of the cell we have understood its structure when we have described as fully as we can the physical relationships that exist between the component molecules. These molecules are, in principle, directly observable and the relationships that exist between them can be ideally expressed in the precise if disembodied language of mathematics. In the case of a biological cell a brief formula or a physical model will tell us more about its structure than a lengthy verbal description which takes account, among other things, of the way such a cell originates.

In the case of Plato's *Republic*, mere description of the observable components will hardly yield the same results. Here the observable data are words, and though it is possible to identify a linguistic structure — that of classical Greek of the early fourth century BC — in some sense equivalent to the structural form found to exist between the component molecules of a cell, the understanding of the book involves something more than the descriptive formulation of that structure. To understand a text involves something more than understanding the syntax and the vocabulary of the language in which it is written. We must understand its meaning and 'meaning' signifies something beyond the grammatical sense of the sentences. Interpretation of texts presupposes knowledge of the relevant syntax and vocabulary but such knowledge is only the necessary first stage in the attempt to grasp meaning. Plato's *Republic* is not a structured succession of words so much as an inherently meaningful argument whose meaning is known by reference to the intentions of its author and the circumstances of its composition, and, as will be shown, the phrase 'circumstances of its composition' involves something more than the particular socio-historical characteristics of the time. Interpretation, the discipline of hermeneutics, draws us implacably toward ontology, a general theory of man's being in the world, and perhaps, if we are successful, to nothing less than the metaphysics of the social world with all that

that implies for our conception of the boundaries of human possibilities.

What is true of a particular literary text is found on examination to be true of every sphere of reality in which man is creatively involved. Certainly the baseline of human existence is the world of nature, but the object of sociological knowledge is the world of social existence, a world that embodies human creativity. One of its characteristics is that it is a world of meaning in which the items of experience have already been organized in accordance with the subjectively meaningful categories of the inhabitants. According to Alfred Schutz this means that a science dealing with human reality has to develop devices foreign to the natural sciences, interpretative or hermeneutic techniques adequate to understanding a realm of reality already structured by human consciousness and effort.

There is [Schutz argues]

> an essential difference in the structure of the thought-objects or mental constructs formed by the social sciences and those formed by the natural sciences. It is up to the natural scientist and to him alone to define, in accordance with the procedural rules of his science, his observational field, and to determine the facts, data and events within it which are relevant for his problem or scientific purpose at hand. Neither are those facts and events preselected, nor is the observational field pre-interpreted. The world of nature, as explored by the natural scientist, does not 'mean' anything to molecules, atoms and electrons. But the observational field of the social scientist — social reality — has a specific meaning and relevance structure for the human beings living, acting and thinking within it. By a series of common-sense constructs they have preselected and pre-interpreted this world which they experience as the reality of their daily lives. It is these thought-objects of theirs which determine their behaviour by motivating it. The thought-objects constructed by the social scientist, in order to grasp this social reality, have to be founded upon the thought-objects constructed by the common-sense thinking of men, living their daily lives within their social world. Thus, the constructs of the social sciences are, so to speak, constructs of the second degree, that is constructs of the constructs made by the actors on the social scene, whose behaviour the social scientist has to observe and to explain in accordance with the procedural rules of his science.[3]

I should emphasize here the degree to which — despite the originality of Schutz's terms and the different ontological assumptions he may have derived from his contact with the work of Edmund Husserl — the theory of second degree constructs is actually a restatement of the central methodological procedure of Aristotelian political science. This point is in the following passage from *The New Science of Politics* by Schutz's long-term correspondent Voegelin:

> When a theorist reflects on his own theoretical situation, he finds himself faced with two sets of symbols: the language symbols that are produced as an integral part of the social cosmion in the process of its self-illumination and the language symbols of political science. Both are related with each other in so far as the second set is developed out of the first one through the process that provisionally was called critical clarification. In the course of this process some of the symbols that occur in reality will be dropped because they cannot be put to any use in the economy of science, while new symbols will be developed in theory for the critically adequate description of symbols that are part of reality. . . . When Aristotle wrote his *Ethics* and *Politics*, when he constructed his concepts of the *polis,* of the constitution, the citizen, the various forms of government, of justice, of happiness, etc., he did not invent these terms and endow them with arbitrary meanings; he took rather the symbols which he found in his social environment, surveyed with care the variety of meanings which they had in common parlance, and ordered and clarified these meanings by the criteria of his theory.[4]

We will return to the parallel between Schutz's and Aristotle's conceptions of the sciences of man. For the moment I will consider the relationship between first and second degree constructs applied to the variety of human motivation, of which the purely cognitive or theoretical priorities of man as scientist are merely a special case.

The world of social reality, or life-world as Schutz (following Husserl) calls it, is one in which the raw data of experience are already meaningfully organized. The criteria of this organization are not those appropriate to natural or social science but those of common sense. To understand the difference between the two we have to recall that whereas for science the primary relationship between man and his environment is cognition, for common sense it is action. Man as scientist pursues knowledge for its own sake, he questions reality in order to learn more about it regardless of whether or not what he investigates presents problems practically touching his conditions of existence. In common sense, reality only becomes problematic when it raises problems for human life. This does not mean that all the problems recognized by common sense are of a purely practical nature. The fact that man organizes his experience in meaningful categories dictates that even in the common-sense universe of the life-world, problems of an apparently theoretical character arise. Advances in insight are commonly triggered by the inability of established systems of meaning, scientific, philosophical or theological, to cope with unforeseen happenings. New items of experience may enter the field of vision and a revision of categories that were formerly adequate may be necessary, or it may be found that there is a clash between different frameworks of meaning present in social consciousness and previously considered compatible. An example is the clash that took place in the nineteenth century between the theological account of man's origins as recounted in *Genesis* and the biological theory of evolution. As a result of this clash the biblical creation story came to be reinterpreted as a symbolic account of the origin of man as a creature peculiarly related to the Divinity.

A meaningful world is one in which man sees his existence as making sense. A world that makes sense is one in which, first, the items of experience are apprehended as existing in intelligible relationship one to another, and, second, man sees himself as intelligibly related to what is about him, primarily the transcendent realities of society and nature. In both spheres what the phenomenologist will interpret as the 'consti-tution' or 'construction' of meaning by the subject will be seen by common sense as the 'discovery' of intrinsic order in the object. And common sense, as we shall see, is not wrong to do so. But for the moment, drawing again on the work of Schutz, let us look at the way the double transcendence of society and nature is experienced and organized.

Society and nature transcend the experiencing individual in a very general and obvious sense. Physically they are not his creation and spiri-tually he is not responsible for the ways in which their component phenomena are apprehended as meaningful.

> Through my natural attitude, [says Schutz] I take the world for granted as my reality. I have to understand it to the extent necessary to come to terms with it, to act within it and upon it and to carry out my projects at hand. In this sense the world is given to my experience and to my interpretation. This interpretation is based upon my stock of previous experiences which in the form of 'knowledge at hand' functions as a scheme of reference. To this knowledge at hand belongs also my knowledge that the world I live in is not a mere aggregate of colored spots, incoherent noises, centers of warm and cold, but a world of well circumscribed objects with definite qualities, objects among which I move, which resist me, and upon which I may act. From the outset these objects are experienced in their typicality: as mountains and stones, trees and animals, and, more specifically, as birds and fishes and snakes.[5]

My stock of knowledge is partly a matter of personal experience in that I recognize certain objects and have certain expectations of them because I have previously encountered them. But this is only a small part of what I know. The life-world is primordially intersubjective and at birth I enter a world which has already been experienced and interpreted by others

'The unique biographical situation in which I find my self within the world at the moment of my existence is only to a very small extent of my own making. I find myself always within an historically given world which, as a world of nature as well as a sociocultural world, had existed before my birth and which will continue to exist after my death.'[6] My experience of the world is structured in two senses. It is biographically structured in the sense that I build up my experience in the time order of my own life and according to my particular position, and it is socially structured in that the particular items encountered are experienced as types whose typical characteristics are made known to me in the social world on the basis of the previous experiences of my contemporaries and predecessors. The scheme of typification is largely something I absorb unconsciously by acquiring a native language which is the typifying medium *par excellence*. Every general noun, such as 'cat' or 'snake', 'storm' or 'music', carries a wealth of expectations built upon previous experience, and these expectations, which may of course have to be revised, are learned as integral elements of the meaning of the words themselves.

The world of nature transcends me in time — pre-existing me and sure to survive me — and in space as well: 'the world within my actual reach carries along the open infinite horizon of my world in potential reach, but to my experiences of these horizons belongs the conviction that each world within potential reach, once transformed into actual reach, will again be surrounded by new horizons, and so on'.[7] To what Schutz calls the 'transcendent infinity' of the natural world corresponds the transcendent infinity of the social world. 'In time, there is the infinite chain of generations which overlap one another; my clan refers to other clans, my tribe to other tribes. . . . My actual social environment refers always to a horizon of potential social environments.'[8] Thus, the actual experience of the social and natural world always refers to potential experience, and, at the limit, to the open horizon of infinity.

The transcendences of Nature and of Society are constitutive elements of my biographical situation and the framework

> 'within which alone I have the freedom of my potentialities, and this means they prescribe the scope of all possibilities for defining my situation. In this sense they are not elements of my situation but determinations of it. In the first sense, I may — even more I have to — take them for granted. In the second sense, I have to come to terms with them. But in either sense, I have to understand the natural world and the social world in spite of their transcendences, in terms of an order of things and events. . . . In the common-sense thinking of everyday life we simply know that Nature and Society represent some kind of order, yet the essence of this order as such is unknowable to us. It reveals itself merely in images by analogical apprehending. But the images once

constituted, are taken for granted, and so are the transcendences to which they refer. . . . We find in our socio-cultural environment itself socially approved systems offering answers for our quest for the unknowable transcendences. Devices are developed to apprehend the disquieting phenomena transcending the world of everyday life in a way analogous to the familiar phenomena within it. This is done by the creation of appresentational references of a higher order, which shall be called *symbols* in contradistinction to the terms 'marks', 'indications', and 'signs'. . . .[9]

Schutz borrows the term 'appresentation' from Husserl to refer to the way in which an item of experience is taken to stand for something else, e.g., a footprint on Robinson Crusoe's island for another human being. 'Signs and Symbols . . . are among the means by which man tries to come to terms with his manifold experiences of transcendency.'[10] 'In all these cases an object, fact or event is not experienced as a "self", but as standing for another object which is not given in immediacy to the experiencing subject. The appresenting member "wakes" or "calls forth" or "evokes" the appresented one.'[11] The life-world is permeated with appresentational references, socially accepted and subjectively satisfying patterns of inference by which an item of experience is known to stand in a particular order with others. Man makes sense of experience by reference to such intelligible connections. He accepts them as existing between items of experience. But at the limit, as we have seen, the order of nature and of society opens out on to, or refers to, transcendent infinity in time and space which goes beyond even potential experience. However much we know by experience, there will always be something beyond, and if we experience social and natural reality as inherently meaningful, the thread of meaning will always reach beyond the realm of experience. The only terms we can use to make sense of this trans-experiential realm are, in a strict sense, symbolic, and the questions of reality and of the nature and validity of symbols are intimately linked because the dimension of reality as experienced opens out on areas where symbolic language is the only available expression we have. This explains the concern with symbolism that distinguishes the most illuminating scholarship in the fields of philosophy and the human sciences today, and leads Mircea Eliade, for instance, to claim:

Symbolic thinking . . . is consubstantial with human existence, it comes before language and discursive reason. The symbol reveals certain aspects of reality — the deepest aspects — which defy any other means of knowledge. Images, symbols and myths are not irresponsible creations of the psyche; they respond to a need and fulfill a function, that of bringing to light the most hidden modalities of being.[12]

How does this bear on our initial question, 'What is social reality'? In the first place it was shown that the world studied by social science is inherently and consciously meaningful to its members in a way that is not true of natural reality. Men strive to understand their existence in a way molecules do not. The reality of the ties that exist between individuals in society is meaningful if each tie is seen as part of an intelligible order of society. In this sense social reality is constituted in terms of individually and socially accepted categories of meaning. But it must be noted that the meaning of social reality is not a matter of arbitrary definition even to the inhabitants. Man is a part of nature and must relate his understanding of himself to what he knows of nature. The area of reality of which he must make sense is not his to define; he must make sense of a limited condition of contingence to what surrounds him. The individual born into society learns to place himself in the order of kinship and hierarchy prevalent in his time and place, and society renders that order meaningful by interpreting it as part of a cosmic or historical order that transcends it. To do this symbols are created which, though drawn from regions of direct experience, refer to dimensions of reality that lie beyond them. Symbolic language completes the constitution of meaning by drawing what is beyond direct experience into intelligible connection with the experienced reality of everyday life. Much at this point depends on how we understand the term 'constitution'. And here there is a danger in the vocabulary which goes back to Husserl's philosophical use of the concept of constitution. Schutz was well aware of the danger but it has not always been avoided by those who have followed him.

At the conclusion of his paper 'The Problem of Transcendental Intersubjectivity in Husserl',[13] Schutz speaks of

> the transformation of sense which the concept of constitution has undergone in the course of the development of phenomenology. At the beginning of phenomenology, constitution meant that clarification of the sense-structure of conscious life, inquiry into sediments in respect of their history, tracing back all *cogitata* to intentional operations of the on-going conscious life. . . . But unobtrusively and almost unaware, it seems to me, the idea of constitution has changed from a clarification of sense-structure, from an explication of the sense of being, into the foundation of the structure of being; it has changed from explication into creation. The disclosure of conscious life becomes a substitute for something of which phenomenology in principle is incapable, *viz*, for establishing an ontology on the basis of the processes of subjective life.

Another philosopher who criticizes the use which Husserl makes of the notion of constitution at the period of the *Cartesian Meditations* is Marvin

Farber. In *The Aims of Phenomenology*[14] he writes: ' "constitution" should not be understood to mean the actual construction of the world, or of any part of it. In the context of a descriptive philosophy of pure experience, the "objective world" is treated as a meaning, an "existence sense". The point is to show how that meaning is "constituted" on the basis of my own "primordial world". The phrase 'primordial world' refers to the basic substratum of experience. But in Husserl's own philosophy that represents an unresolved problem. Is it the life-world of the natural attitude, the common-sense world taken for granted as existing beyond the mind, as the philosopher's late manuscripts suggest? Or is it to be found in the activity of a constituting transcendent subject in whose experience the very notion of reality finds its source, as suggested by the painstaking analyses of the *Cartesian Meditations*? Schutz thought that the tenor of Husserl's philosophy favoured the latter view. Though he took the concept of the life-world from it, he rejected Husserl's attempt to trace its reality to the level of transcendental subjectivity. This was necessary because Schutz held that intersubjectivity was an irreducible characteristic of social reality, and intersubjectivity, the presence of others in subjective experience, presented a problem which appeared to be insoluble from Husserl's standpoint.

Because Schutz does not conceive the constitutive function as anything more than an organizing or sense-giving process, he avoids the toils of Husserl's idealism. But by carrying the notion of constitution over from transcendental phenomenology to the analysis of social reality, he brings into the field an equivocal concept which had already misled its originator, and can all too easily mislead the unwary social scientist in the same idealist and subjectivist direction. The result is a definition of social reality entirely in terms of the sense-endowing procedures of the inhabitants that takes no account of the intrinsic nature of those objects and situations out of which sense must be made.

Take Farber's words again: ' "constitution" should not be understood to mean the actual construction of the world . . . the "objective world" is treated as a meaning. . . . The point is to show how that meaning is "constituted" on the basis of my own "primordial world".' For the individual in society the primordial world is the life-world complete with common-sense 'recipe' knowledge and socially accepted beliefs. For the society in space and time it is nothing less than the totality of the existing universe, transcending common experience, out of which meaning is to be constituted by discovering intelligibly necessary and existentially possible structures connecting the known with the unknown realms of being. Such a discovery can only be articulated by creating a complex of symbols, whose components adequately render the items of experience while suggestively linking them in meaningful order. If experienced reality is not self-explanatory in a meaningful way, such languages show why this is so, and integrate the known realm with one that is unknown but whose reality must be accepted if the meaning within the known realm is to hold. When this is understood, it is clear why the confrontation with transcendent reality represented by religion is such a permanent feature of social reality. 'Ultimately', wrote the Thomist theologian, Father Garrigou-Lagrange, 'the choice is between God and radical absurdity.' At the limit of meaning the terms of religion are a substitute for silence and silence will be seen as marking the ultimate failure of meaning in the world. As a term, 'God' conveys, though does not describe, what must be if our experience of reality is as meaningful as we take it to be.

There is another, more immediately relevant, point which Marvin Farber's words suggest. If constitution is rightly understood as a constitution of meaning rather than, in the literal sense, a construction of reality, the sociologist must bear in mind the natural, existential baseline on which meaning is built or from which it is drawn. The natural world provides the limits within which the constitution of meaning can take place. The items that are to be meaningfully organized are not themselves produced by the meaning-endowing process. This has, of itself, no ontological consequences. What we make sense of is given us to discover before we actually begin to do so. Thus the question 'What is social reality?' is wider than, 'How is social reality constituted?' This 'is' of the first is not reducible to the 'constituted' of the second. The first takes account of a physical and metaphysical dimension of which the second asks nothing. Forgetfulness of this can lead to the sort of conclusions that such 'ethnomethodologists' as Harold Garfinkel have been taken to imply; for instance, that the roots of sex and gender distinctions in society lie in conventional matters of social definition, rather than in physiology.

To illustrate this I return to Schutz and his view of intersubjectivity as the defining feature of social reality. We cannot answer our question about social reality by an analysis of the life-world and its structures which is content to discover its unity or coherence at the level of intersubjectivity. The analysis must be extended so that the real, existential or cosmological ground of intersubjectivity can be brought into the picture. What we experience must be understood in itself, beyond or before the descriptive analysis of the way meaning comes to be shared. Only at that level will we be able to ask how far concepts and symbols are determined in their content by a reality whose nature is unaltered by the play of the mind, and, thus, of the way the baseline of nature relates to the meaning structures of society.

In a much-quoted sentence from the conclusion of his paper 'Husserl's Importance for the Social Sciences', Schutz remarks that 'the empirical social sciences will find their true foundation not in transcendental phenomenology, but in the constitutive phenomenology of the natural attitude.' He continues:

Husserl's signal contribution to the social sciences consists neither in his unsuccessful attempt to solve the problem of the constitution of the transcendental intersubjectivity within the reduced egological sphere, nor in his unclarified notion of empathy as the foundation of understanding, nor finally, in his interpretation of communities and societies as subjectivities of a higher order the nature of which can be described eidetically, but rather in the wealth of his analyses pertinent to problems of the *Lebenswelt* and designed to be developed into a philosophical anthropology.[15]

Now, we know from the late essay 'Symbol, Reality and Society' (1955) that Schutz considered one of the main problems of a philosophical anthropology to be the explication of the types of symbolization found universally in human societies.

How is it possible? [he asks] that an object, event or fact within the reality of our daily life is coupled with an idea which transcends our experience of our daily life? This problem can be approached on two different levels. There are first sets of appresentational references which are universal and can be used for symbolization because they are rooted in the human condition. It is a problem of philosophical anthropology to study these sets of appresentational references. Secondly, the particular forms of symbolic systems as developed by the various cultures in different periods must be investigated. This is the problem of cultural anthropology and of the history of ideas.[16]

Drawing on the work of other scholars, Schutz then proceeds to analyse briefly how universal symbols arise in an experience of the transcendence of the universe common to all men. Man sees himself as the centre of a system of coordinates, and groups the objects of his environment in terms of 'above and underneath', 'before and behind', 'right and left'. Universally, the earth is below and the sky above, and analogies can be established between what is above, what below and what takes place at the level of social life.

Sun, moon and stars rise and set for all men in opposite directions which are to everyone 'marks' for finding his bearings. But the four cardinal points of the compass so ascertained have also their symbolic connotations, because they are connected with the change between day and night, light and darkness, being awake and asleep, the visible and invisible, the coming-to-be and the passing-away. The life cycle of men — birth, childhood, adolescence, manhood, old age, death — has its analogy in the cycle of the seasons and the cycle of vegetative and animal life which is equally important for farming, fishing and animal husbandry, and is in turn correlated to the motions of the heavenly bodies. Thus, the cosmos, the individual, and the community form a unit and are equally subject to the universal forces which govern all events. Man has to understand these forces and, because he cannot dominate them, to conjure or to appease them. To do so, however, is not the business of the isolated individual, it is the concern of the whole community and its organization.[17]

In his analysis of what he calls the 'paramount reality' of the world of work, which is characterized by a maximum degree of attention permitting the individual to 'gear into' the surrounding social and natural world, Schutz insists on the defining or delimiting character of external reality. Here, in complementary fashion, he draws attention to how symbols are largely conditioned by a transcendent world of infinite dimensions to which man is irretrievably related by material and cognitive need. In so far as these needs and dimensions are universal determinants of the human condition, it is possible to judge the adequacy of different symbolic systems in relation to them. A system which ignores material limitations will be inadequate in these terms, as will one which refuses to admit the finite character of human knowledge and the infinity of the realm beyond. We must conclude that an answer to the question of social reality will be found not in the realm of intersubjective social definitions alone, but in the character of that universal reality by which such definitions can be judged and on which the common character of these definitions is based.

An objective science of social reality has, then, a task of interpretation which encompasses several levels. It must give a true account of the systems of meanings by which men in society make sense of their lives. Then it must seek to understand the variations between such systems by reference to the particular historical circumstances of the societies in which they arise. It must relate these different systems to universal symbolic patterns of the type suggested by Schutz. And, finally, it must refer these universal symbolisms to the character of the human condition as rooted in a reality that can neither be dreamed nor defined away. It must move through intersubjectivity to the objective world of which we are conscious and on which the work of consciousness builds. To use Paul Ricoeur's terms, an interpretation of social reality cannot rest before it has shown the way in which 'my world', or 'our world', is always an aspect of 'the world'. To recognize that, while the languages of symbolic understanding are man-made, the problems with which they cope are not is important in this process. It leads us to a re-evaluation of the common-sense belief in symbolic religious and metaphysical meaning structures as discoveries of truths about the universe. We can admit the phenomenological insight into such structures as social constructions while justifying their common-sense status as the articulate forms of insight into reality. It is the distinction between the man-made character of the languages of religion, metaphysics and, for that matter, natural science, and the existentially-given problems which they confront that enables us to do so.

An analogy with the realm of artistic creation will help here. Eliseo Vivas maintains that the understanding of the work of an artist involves its interpretation under two aspects, that of creation and that of discovery.

> How [he asks] shall we resolve the contradiction involved in the claim that the artist *creates* novel objects and that he *discovers* the hidden reality of our practical, common-sense world? The contradiction is only apparent, not real, since the two assertions were made from different points of view. From the standpoint of the world of experience, the spatio-temporal world of culture and history, of which the poet and his reader are part, the artist *creates* meanings, values and fitting form. But these values, meanings and their form subsist prior to the making of the poem. The act of making is thus a *discovery* that takes place as the poet in his making goes beyond the matter of his experience; the discovery takes place when he makes the effort to extricate the import and order of his experience and body it forth in language. From the external point of view, there is novelty in his product, and spontaneity is involved in the process of making. From the standpoint of the artist, however, we grasp a different aspect of the process, since what the artist does is not to invent something new, but to extricate out of the subject matter at hand its proper structure or order.[18]

Vivas' analysis of the dual significance of artistic work can be extended to the whole range of the human world of meaning. Any particular theological, metaphysical, social or natural scientific theory is open to interpretation as a human creation. But we will never understand the power of any theory to convince (any more than we will understand the impact of Eliot's *The Waste Land),* nor the reason why one will be found preferable to another, unless we also understand it as the articulation of a discovery about the structure or order of reality. The terms employed in the theory are not spoken by nature, but the realities to which they refer, even the reality of a realm of being beyond direct experience, are present in the structure of experience itself. Experience always refers to that which goes beyond its immediate content. The existence of any child entails recognition of the existence of its parents.

Social reality, including the meaning constructs it embodies, is rooted in man's experience of his existence as a limited being who must, for his survival, 'gear into' the transcendent reality of society and nature. He encounters reality as a limiting realm that imposes material tasks upon him and, at the same time, seems to demand explanation in terms of meaning. The space for meaningful interpretation is delimited by reality itself. Man's meaning constructs only prove adequate to the case, and thus subjectively meaningful, when they take account of the full range of experience. And, at the limit, this range will extend beyond what can be known directly. A symbolic account of reality, may, for one reason or another, fail. In that case its inadequacy may be brought to light either by pointing to realms of experience it does not cover, or by showing the manner in which it prevents us raising questions which would reveal its limitations. Eric Voegelin does this in his essay 'The Eclipse of Reality' which he contributed to the volume *Phenomenology and Social Reality* published as a memorial to the work of Schutz.[19] Perhaps Schutz himself would have developed his analysis in the same direction had he lived to write the philosophical anthropology which he seems to have had in mind. As it is, the emphasis in his writings is overwhelmingly on the constitutive or creative rather than the interpretative or hermeneutic aspect of establishing meaning in the world. This emphasis, stressing the subjective level of individual and social articulation of meaning over the objective level of the human condition and its limitations, leaves the way open for conventionalists and subjectivist developments of his teaching at odds with his intentions revealed in the passages I have discussed.

Toward the end of *The Phenomenology of the Social World* Schutz concludes that 'All social sciences are objective meaning-contexts of subjective meaning-contexts.'[20] In giving a true account of the inherent meaning structures of a society, the social scientist depicts social reality as it truly is. Here I have suggested the necessity of supplementing this level of interpretation with an account of the objective material and cognitive setting in which subjective meaning is grounded. Only if we do this can we answer the question: 'What is social reality?'

2 The Foundation of Interpretative Sociology

I want to pursue the question of social reality raised above and, more specifically, to throw some light on the status of sociology as a human science and the sort of understanding which social scientific analysis can provide. First let me clarify the chapter's title which is deliberately ambiguous. The ambiguity inheres in the meaning of the term 'foundation', which might be taken in two different senses. On the one hand 'foundation' might mean the historic founding of a self-conscious discipline of sociology in the nineteenth century and particularly Max Weber's effort to reconcile the idealist tradition of sympathetic understanding of human action, *verstehen*, with the rigours of causal explanation on the model of the natural sciences. On the other, 'foundation' could refer to the founding, or grounding, of sociological explanations in other, more basic, levels of interpretation which belong to the field of philosophical anthropology, the general theory of man, and ontology, the theory of reality or being as such. Though, as the first chapter should suggest, I believe the latter meaning to be the more significant, the very possibility of such a founding is a matter of dispute, and the reason for this dispute can be found in the anti-ontological character of both currents of thought that Weber sought to reconcile, which we may designate 'positivism' and 'historical idealism' respectively. The problem of intellectual history involved in Weber's attempt to draw the two strands together, and, more particularly, the often unnoticed common ancestry of positivism and historical idealism could, therefore, throw considerable light on the reason that the problem of the ontological reference of sociological theories and explanations remains unresolved to this day. To put it baldly: the nature of social reality and the foundation of objectivity in social scientific explanation remain the problems they are because neither positivism nor historical idealism provides us with an adequate notion of reality. Consequently neither can correctly answer the ontological question, and an interpretative sociology, like Weber's, which is anchored philosophically in a conciliation of the two, will, at the philosophical level, do no better. What this means is that however much light the investigations of such a sociology may throw on the object of study, which in the hands of a man of Weber's perceptiveness is great indeed, the investigator will not, within the terms of his approach, be able to give an adequate account of why his conclusions should be regarded as true.

17

Chiefly this chapter is an exercise in critical clarification, a work of theory rather than a study in the history of ideas. I shall proceed by examining what a number of theorists have said about the central problem in order to see where an adequate conceptualization of social reality and a valid notion of sociological explanation may be found. An examination of the sources of Weber's thought and even a sufficient exposition and critique of his positions must await another occasion. Nevertheless, it is important to say something of the defects of the two principal traditions which nourished his work if only to justify the statement that neither positivism nor historical idealism provides sociology with an adequate notion of reality. The procedures and immanent logic of a science ought to be a function of the nature of the reality which it studies, and a defective conception of social reality will give rise to a defective notion of social science.

Actually, despite the differences between them, both positivism and historical idealism are rooted in a Kantian conception of the relationship between knowing subject and known object.[1] In a sense they can be taken to represent alternative paths forward from the position left by Kant's so-called 'Copernican' revolution in epistemology. Kant taught, in opposition to the scepticism of David Hume, that an objective science of the external world was possible not because the mind could have any ultimate insight into the nature of reality in itself but because reality is always structured by categories (time, space, causality) imposed by the mind itself. The world of experience, the phenomenal world, is already structured by the experiencing subject. Questions concerning another, noumenal, world behind this realm of experience are unanswerable and, anyway, irrelevant to science, for they refer to a realm which is beyond experience and cannot impinge on it in any way. Positivism and historical idealism both develop from this position and, even when they disown Kant's own teachings, remain inwardly bound by the character of the Kantian problematic.

Positivism in all its many forms is Kantian in teaching that we must forego questions touching on the problem of the nature of reality itself. All we can know are the phenomena of the world as experienced and primarily we know them as observed objects. Only in so far as we can record regular connections between these observables can we speak of the world as ordered. In this view causality, for instance, becomes no more than a function of statistical generalization, and we are bound, as far as possible, to explain observed phenomena in terms of each other; in Durkheim's terms, to explain social facts by other social facts. Social reality, conceived by positivism, is a reality of factual variables whose correlations, when formulated in sociological 'laws', are conceived as causal determinants of all that happens in society. We can accept Anthony Giddens' point that Durkheim's celebrated injunction 'treat social facts as things' is a methodological injunction rather than an ontological proposition, but the concept of human actions as in some sense caused by the external environment, in a way analogous to the movements of dead matter, is implied in the positivist position and this has ontological implications.[2] Thus positivism systematically ignores, or at least underestimates, the extent to which social reality is a realm of more or less rational individuals freely choosing lines of action in accord with personal systems of relevance and subjective estimates of the options available. This observation does not open the way to a retreat from scientific objectivity in sociological explanation, except in so far as science is defined in a rigidly positivist way as the delineation of invariable laws among facts assumed to be unvarying. Nor does it imply that actions are decided upon and projects formulated in a vacuum. Rather, the reintroduction into science of the apparently subjective realm of reasons and free choices is meant to lead to a deeper objectivity than positivism recognizes, an objectivity tied to the ontological knowledge of the nature of man and his relationship to the surrounding universe. We might say that man is, in a certain sense, caused to have reasons and purposes and that this is what is meant when we say, following Aristotle, that man is a rational animal. He is caused, by his circumstances, to make decisions, and, by his nature, to make them in a certain conscious way, but the content of the particular decisions he reaches is not in any way a simple, dependent function of the cause, though habit and external circumstances will usually predispose him to choose one course rather than another. We may formulate this by saying that consciousness is neither passive nor purely or irresponsibly active; rather, it is reactive in the sense that it reacts creatively to the possibilities of the context. Only this formulation does justice to the way human beings respond creatively to the discovered problems of human existence.

If positivism develops through emphasis on the phenomenalist, antimetaphysical side of Kantianism, historical idealism grows from the same root emphasizing the subjectivist possibilities of the teaching. Take Kant's theory of knowledge, remove from it the insistence on the universality of the categories by which the mind of man orders the world, and you have the core of the historical idealist position. The historical idealist conceives social reality as a manifestation of the activity of the human spirit. This spirit manifests itself differently at different times and in different individuals and peoples. Thus the understanding of another man and age is conceived as a task different in kind from the explanation of natural phenomena. Causal analysis is out of place and must, in the sciences of man, be replaced by a form of empathy with another or at least a sympathetic understanding of the immanent logic of the other's position. The historical idealist overestimates the differences between men and ages because he underestimates the importance of the relatively unchanging cosmological context of human action, the extent to which *our* world is always an aspect of *the* world. As a result of this, historical idealism exaggerates the differences between the human and the natural sciences and their modes of explanation. The human and the natural sciences are neither identical in their procedures nor wholly unlike. Properly seen, the natural is the fundamental component of the social and in all circumstances constitutes the limiting framework for cultural creation.

Historical idealism interprets culture in isolation from the suprahistorical and natural or cosmological elements of the human condition. Thus it overestimates the degree of autonomy involved in cultural creation. This is the opposite mistake of positivism, which when consistent always tends toward determinism, and though it produces a more subjectively appealing view of social reality, it is one that is equally defective. In relation to the problem of social scientific explanation, both approaches exclude elements which seem essential to the attainment of a full sense of what is involved in human action. Positivism does this because it involves a notion of causal analysis which leaves no place for the play of human rationality and creativity, and historical idealism because it leaves out of account the common ground that natural and human sciences share, which means, in the end, the world itself. Luckily, nothing compels us to be either positivists or historical idealists. There are other positions, and they are ones that turn out to be much more compelling. Take, for example, the case which Hans Jonas makes in his essay 'Change and Permanence'.[3] Though Professor Jonas's prime focus is on the interpretation of a human reality that is past, his observations are also relevant to a sociological or anthropological understanding of the present. Jonas begins by pointing out that we do as a matter of fact understand words describing the experience of others, even when that experience is transmitted to us from a remote time and place and is without direct equivalent in our own lives. We can understand the grief of Achilles over the death of his friend Patroclus and his anger against his slayer, Hector, 'without being Achilles ourselves, ever having loved a Patroclus and dragged a Hector through the dust. Socrates passes a life in discourse, examines opinions, asks what virtue and knowledge are, makes himself the gadfly of Athens in obedience to the gods' command, and dies for it. Do we understand this? Yes we do, without ourselves being capable of such a life and such a death.'[4] And yet, though we understand these matters, do we understand them correctly? The words are meaningful to us but can we know that the meaning they have for us is the same as that they had for those who first spoke them and to whom they were addressed? As Jonas notes, these are not problems peculiar to the interpretation of historical texts but extend even to the understanding of the next fellow man, something which is well recognized by Schutz in *The Phenomenology of the Social World*.

Three logical possibilities underlie the solutions that are offered to the problem of understanding the expressions of one man by another. The first is based on the claim that man has a nature that is the same at all times and places, and that therefore the full range of human experience is comprehensible, because any man can imaginatively reproduce within himself the experience of another. This theory of understanding rests on an ontological theory making specific claims about the constancy of human nature. Against it may be set the view, 'that *what* "man" is at any time is the product of his own *de facto* existing and of the choices made therein; and, further, that the scope of his existing, even the kind and content of the choices open to it are, in their turn, predetermined by the facticity of spatio-temporal place, by the circumstance and accident of the historical situation; and, finally, that each such situation is unique.'[5] This position, which is as much an ontological doctrine as the other, does not logically entail the possibility of understanding with the underpinning of the theory of a constant human nature, but it does not exclude the possibility of correct interpretation. Thus, on its basis, may be created either a theory of human understanding or a view wholly sceptical of the possibility. For who is to pronounce that understanding must always involve the understanding of like by like? And therefore, though the radical mutability view of human nature can give rise to a total scepticism concerning the possibility of understanding others correctly, it may also found a claim for the viability of a science of that which is radically other than oneself.

Hans Jonas sees merit in all three positions but maintains that though the truth of each is no more than partial, the doctrine of constancy in human nature is more fundamental than the other, being covertly assumed even by those who seem to deny it; 'for they predicate their negation . . . not of an empty, arbitrary x, but of Man, as something attributable to him uniquely and in distinction from the animal, which is captive in each instance to its specific essence; this very negativity thus is claimed for man as an "essential" property.'[6] This argument recalls Etienne Gilson's criticism of Sartre's view of man as a being having no determinate nature because what he is depends only upon the choices he makes in the course of his existence, that man is a being whose existence precedes his essence and is 'nothing else but what he makes himself'. As Gilson says, 'What then does one mean in speaking here of man? If we mean the individual, I admit that I define myself by my successive free moral choices; this indeed is the essence of personal morality, but I can only define myself within the limits of an essence, that of man, which it is not within my power to create.'[7] Gilson goes on to show that either Sartre's position is meaningless or his use of essence is entirely different from what we usually understand when we talk of human essence or nature. In neither case is it an argument against the view of a constant human nature.

Yet the doctrine of constancy in human nature, though fundamental, does not bring the whole truth to light, and the passage in which Jonas discusses the contributions of each of the three positions to a more adequate perspective deserves to be quoted in full.

The doctrine of the one, permanent human nature contains the truth that an inalienable kinship links the children of man across the farthest distances of history and the greatest diversities of culture; that this common ground supports and holds together and explains all the manifoldness which unpredictably comes forth from it; and that only with this as a basis is history possible at all, as well as the understanding of it. The doctrine of man's fundamental mutability and actual changing, and of the uniqueness of each product of change, contains the truth that the particularization of humanity in the different cultures, and again in the progress of each culture, and again in the individuals sharing it, produces genuine and unpredictable otherness; that consequently the "knowledge of the like" must transcend itself; and that — taking off from the basis of the like — an understanding of the widely different is possible and must be striven for. *How* it is possible, is as yet an open question. Finally, the doctrine of the necessary failure of all understanding contains the truth that the interpreter indeed imports himself into the interpreted, inevitably alienating it from itself and assimilating it to his *own* being and also, that every advance leaves an indelible remainder of the non-understood, which recedes before it into infinity.[8]

This passage clears the way for Jonas's discussion of the nature of human understanding and historical understanding in particular. Throughout he stresses the outward facing nature of consciousness, arguing that we must reject the Cartesian perspective according to which we achieve knowledge of other minds only by analogical inference from consciousness of self. If anything the reverse is true. Knowledge of our own minds, even consciousness of mind as such, is

a function of acquaintance with other minds. Knowledge of inwardness as such, whether one's own or that of others, is based on communication with a whole environment which determines, certainly codetermines decisively, even what will be found in eventual introspection. Since we begin life as infants (a fact philosophers so easily forget), coming into a world already peopled with adults, the particular "I" to-be is at first far more the receiver than the giver in this communication. In the course of it, the rudimentary inwardness that is to be "I" evolves by gradually beholding from the address, utterance and conduct of others what inward possibilities there are and making them its own.[9]

Animal life is expressive and its expressions are directly given to perception. That this extends beyond the range of the human is clear to anyone who has seen devotion or fear on the face of a dog; but within humanity its range is greater and its content more highly differentiated. We understand others not because we have any sort of 'hot-line' to another's consciousness, nor, usually, by analogy with our own experiences, for we often understand that which we have never actually experienced. Understanding rests far more on sensed potentiality for a certain experience than on actual experience.

> To 'know love by love' is not to infer, from my own experience of the feeling of love, what is probably going on in someone else. I may first be awakened by *Romeo and Juliet* to the potentialities of love, by the tale of Thermopylae to the beauty of sacrificial heroism. This is itself an experience, showing me undreamt-of possibilities of my own soul — or rather, of 'the soul' — possibilities that may or may not become actualities of my own experience. *This experience of the potential, mediated by symbols, is precisely what is meant by 'understanding'* .... The knowledge of other minds thus rests on the ground of the common humanity of men — in such a manner, however, that the common ground is effective, not by supplying parallels between what *is there* in the self and the other, but by allowing the voice of the other to call on the possibilities that lie latent in the soul of man or can be elicited from his nature.[10]

Jonas then analyses what he means by the common humanity of man. In the first place there are the biological constants that are so taken for granted that they are rarely mentioned in explanation. These are the needs of the body for food, water and sleep, the succession of childhood, adulthood and old age, the mortality of the body and the duality of the sexes. To recognize the importance of these unspoken assumptions we need only consider the difficulty of explaining the problems involved in Napoleon's retreat from Moscow to a being from another planet, who received sustenance directly from the atmosphere, could fly effortlessly through the air without artificial aids, and needed sleep for no more than three hours a year. A history teacher summoned to teach the rudiments of earth history to the offspring of such a being would soon realize the extent to which these biological constants are assumed in everything he has hitherto said. But the field of constancy is certainly not exhausted at this level.

Passing from the biological to the cultural level, we find the products of man to be just as revealing of the community of human nature. Discovered human artifacts belong to three categories typified respectively by the tool, the image and the tomb. These categories, Jonas argues, primevally foreshadow the later development of physics, art and metaphysics. Tool, image and tomb each points in its fashion to constancy in the nature of man's relationship to the world:

> The *tool* (any utensil, including weapon and vessel) tells us that here a being, compelled by his needs to deal with matter, serves these needs in artificially mediated ways originating from invention and open to

further invention. The *image* tells us that here a being, using tools on matter for an immaterial end, represents to himself the contents of his perception, plays with their variations and augments them by new shapes — thus generating another object-world of representation beyond the physical objects of his need and its direct satisfaction. The *tomb* tells us that here a being, subject to mortality, meditates on life and death, defies appearance and elevates his thought. These are basic forms in which man, in uniquely human fashion, answers and transcends what is an unconditional given for man and animal alike. With the tool he surpasses physical necessity through invention; with the image, passive perception through representation and imagination; with the tomb, inescapable death through faith and piety. All three, in their transcending function, are divergent modes of a freedom shared by us with the bygone makers of those artifacts and all who came between them and us; so shared they can serve as universal "coordinates" of understanding for the whole course of human history.[11]

Up to this point we have not mentioned language, perhaps the most important thing that distinguishes humankind from the rest of the animal kingdom and without which the other unique traits of humanity could never have come to be. The language of another human being, as spoken and written, is potentially understandable both as expressive of man and significative of the world. Thus the understanding of an alien language rests, beyond any immediate linguistic affinities it may have with our own, on the constancies of the nature of man and the surrounding reality in which he participates. But language does much more than express the constant elements in the human condition, it is also, as Jonas reminds us, the vehicle of historicity; the medium through which, above the base ground of our common humanity, the unique historical existence of each culture is constituted. Within language we find,

> on the one hand, the almost secret, primordial words or coded insights, in which a particular culture from the outset articulates its posture toward the world, its basic grasp of reality that preconditions all the rest — what we may call the animating spirit of a universe of speech which opens up, and at the same time delimits, its possible range of truth; and, on the other hand, the peaks of poetry and speculation, in which this primordial life of the words comes to its highest (but still deceptive) lucidity of symbolic and conceptual expression.[12]

These, the highest and lowest reaches of language, are, says Jonas, the most historical of phenomena and therefore those most difficult to grasp. In them the constants on which understanding rests are most veiled or attenuated. Employing the terminology of Voegelin, we may say that the most compact of symbols and the most differentiated of concepts are, of all human expressions, those hardest of access. The wealth of meaning they potentially convey bursts the seam of the most sensitive interpretation. As Ricoeur shows in *The Symbolism of Evil*, even a primary symbol as universal as the stain symbolic of defilement, sin and guilt presents almost insurmountable problems to the would-be analyst. In its very compactness or density it holds together primary insights into the relationship between man and his context that threaten to be lost in forgetfulness or contradiction the moment we try to translate them into the rational discourse of contemporary hermeneutics.[13] At the other end of the scale, a masterpiece of analytical speculation like Aristotle's *Metaphysics* poses problems almost equally great. In this case they are the result not of preanalytical density but of the very lucidity of analysis and sophistication of concepts. In becoming reified in the rigidity of scientific or philosophic terminology, these threaten to bar our way back to the original experience of being that sparked the flame of speculation to begin with. Both Heidegger and Voegelin note that the very success of a particular knot of concepts may obscure the nature of the experience which first gave rise to them. Furthermore, we should note that the wealth of meaning contained in both primordial symbols and sophisticated speculation will usually exceed even the understanding of those with whom the expressions originate, a point not without significance for present disputes concerning the explanation of human action. No one is aware of the full ramifications of what he says, which is why new insights may often be expressed in well established vocabulary. This is particularly true of those expressions through which man tries to articulate the fundamentals of his existence in relation to the cosmos.

Let me here state a position that is, I think, implied by Jonas's argument and which the rest of this chapter will try to confirm. To interpret a human expression, whether statement, text, rite or action, it is necessary not only to identify its immanent logic, which is sometimes all it consciously means to the man who says it or participates in it, but also to situate it in context, which means, ultimately, the cosmological context of man as participant in universal reality. In the last analysis, then, *verstehen*, as a method, refers back to the ontological clarification of the being of the actor in the world. This is the implicit ontological reference of every social scientific explanation, and, once understood, it enables us to avoid the conventionalism and relativism which mars certain strands of sociology influenced by phenomenology or the late philosophy of Wittgenstein which are, otherwise, extremely valuable efforts to comprehend the intentional structure of human existence. For instance, Peter Winch's view that meaningful action is action which is rule-governed and that we have explained an action when we have identified the socially sanctioned rule to which it is oriented, will be seen as inadequate in so far as it fails to refer such rules back to the character of the cosmos out of which rules try to make sense or to which they orient man in a meaningful way. In his late philosophy Wittgenstein draws on the analogy between the rules of language and the rules of a game; but this analogy becomes misleading in the human sciences if we forget that in the game of life, though men set some of the rules, individually or collectively, the object of the game is mysterious and the parameters of the board are not the work of any human agent. Systems of meaning change, and can sometimes be judged as more or less adequate, precisely because under certain conditions we are able to see a little more of the board than before or at least to read its pattern more clearly.[14]

Similarly, in the phenomenological camp, we may criticize Michael Phillipson's statement: 'The ontological presuppositions of phenomenological sociology . . . derived from the descriptions of phenomenological philosophy, posit a social world constituted and sustained through meaning, so that the prime characteristic of its model of man is man's meaning-giving ability.'[15] This too must be judged a faulty ontology to the extent that it fails to take into account the natural parameters within which meaning is constituted. Social reality, and even what any given society may count as real, is not as much a matter of convention as Phillipson suggests. Social reality is ineradicably founded in natural reality, the reality of natures, which means the nature of man and the nature of everything that he encounters. Interpretative sociology, as the disciplined study of that realm, must penetrate the layers of conventional social meaning and the particular symbols of society to reach that fundamental level. In other words, it must achieve understanding of the being of man, in the sense both of his nature and his ways of being in the world, in order that it may explain his conduct and make sense of his symbolic expressions. At this level too the analysis of social institutions finds its ultimate source of explanation, for institutions like linguistic symbols are a variety of human creative response to the range of naturally given possibilities. They are created in the spaces which cognitive and material need reveals. To use the formulation borrowed from Vivas's aesthetics, they are discovered as more or less appropriate solutions to the cognitive and material problems men face in their efforts to come to terms with reality.

What, we may now ask, is the significance of the implicit ontological reference of every sociological explanation for our view of interpretation, or *verstehen*, as it is meant in the Weberian phrase 'interpretative sociology'? This can best be seen by glancing briefly at the notion of *verstehen* as found in the tradition of German social science from Dilthey to Schutz. The changes which the theory of interpretation undergoes in this span reveal a steady disengagement of the concept of *verstehen* from the scientifically untenable view that correct interpretation involves direct empathy with another mind. I must stress that this turn in the chapter does not amount to a shift from the perspective of theory to that of the history of ideas. From the latter perspective what I shall say would be utterly insufficient though not, I hope, misleading. In order to focus more clearly on the present interest in the critical clarification of concepts, I must forego the empirical task of rendering the history of a particular development in human thinking, in which the arguments of 'X' were actually developed as a direct answer to the perceived inadequacies of those put forward by 'Y' and 'Z', as Weber developed his position in response to those of Roscher and Knies. Instead, I shall isolate what seem the most significant moments in this story to illustrate the trend away from psychic empathy and towards interpretative procedures which point to the sort of ontology I consider necessary to the attainment of a valid perspective. For this purpose the significant moments are the early position of Dilthey, Weber's distinction between observational and motivational understanding, and the criticism of that distinction by Schutz.

The early thought of Dilthey represents an extremely interesting attempt both to distinguish *verstehen* as the method uniquely suited to the human sciences from the method of causal explanation suitable to the natural sciences, *erklären*, and to give it an equal degree of objectivity. According to Dilthey, *verstehen* involves a direct understanding of the consciousness of the other. This can be accomplished by psychological re-enactment or imaginative reconstruction of the other's experience. The human world is one of creative freedom to which causal analysis would be inappropriate, and there is therefore a problem of how can we adequately conceptualize the form of understanding that is appropriate to it? This was to remain Dilthey's life-long preoccupation, even though the early formulation of *verstehen* as involving the imaginative reliving of another's experience failed to satisfy him because it could not be rationally confirmed. Who, after all, can say whether or not we have truly re-enacted another's psychic experience? The insolubility of the problem led Dilthey in other directions which were to culminate in his influential essay 'The Development of Hermeneutics' first published in 1900.[16] I shall return to it later in the book but for the moment turn to Max Weber.

In contrast to Dilthey, Weber rejected the view that there is a logical gap between the methods of the natural and the human sciences. According to Weber, interpretative understanding of meaning and motive is not an alternative to causal explanation but rather its precondition for the sciences of man. Weber's view, as expressed in the essay on the problem of irrationality in the work of Roscher and Knies, is that 'the historian's "interpretative" research in terms of motives is causal assessment in absolutely the same logical sense as causal interpretation of any parti-cular individual event in nature. For their aim is to postulate "sufficient" grounds (at least as a hypothesis), in just the same way as is necessarily the case with research into natural phenomena, if it is concerned with indivi-dual components.'[17] Thus, the logical identity which Weber maintains between the methods of the natural and human sciences is based on the assumption that the more or less rational motives of men are in fact the causes of their actions. But Weber supplements such motivational analysis with what he calls observational understanding of acts whose meaning is immediately transparent to the observer. His famous example is the action of a woodcutter, in which the bodily actions of the actor are taken as immediately signifying a particular type of comprehensible activity without any element of psychic empathy or motivational understanding being involved in the process; or, in the simplest terms, that to see a man chopping wood is to understand what he is doing.

This view has common sense on its side but it conceals numerous ambiguities and difficulties. On the one hand, Weber does not make it clear what the relationship is between the meaning an action has for the observer and the meaning it has for the actor: on the other, does not the very use of the category 'woodcutter' imply a frame of reference that necessarily precedes so-called observational understanding? How, in other words, can we observe an actor and know him to be a woodcutter unless we have some grasp of the type he represents and the typical actions that 'woodcutters' engage in? After all, it is only because we are familiar with the conventions of theatre that we know that there is no need to leap to the rescue of an old lady about to be strangled before our eyes on the stage. And our understanding of what is at stake when a man announces his intention to saw a girl in half will be different depending on whether or not we know him to be a conjurer. A person from a society in which theatre and conjuring were unknown would certainly have a very different 'observational understanding' of these actions from the average British holidaymaker. The apparent 'transparency' of the actions turns out to rest on a usually unconsidered familiarity with patterns of activity typical of a society we know well.

Schutz's analysis of Weber's methodological concepts in *The Phenomenology of the Social World* aims to clarify just these problems. Schutz concludes that whatever may be the place of observational understanding in everyday life, social scientific interpretation is always of a less immediate type. The very anonymity and generality of sociological explanation renders impossible the sort of empathic communion that may be achieved between intimates, and the consciously scientific character of the understanding for which the social scientist aims invalidates the tacit assumptions on which the immediacy of what we think of as 'observational understanding' always rests. The sociologist's task is to discover and describe the typical meaning patterns that operate in a given society and to refer individual actions back to the appropriate pattern, but he cannot, as a social scientist, know for certain whether in any particular case the likely motive was in fact the meaning-reference of the action for the actor. Thus, his task is not to concern himself with the ultimately unknowable psychic processes of the individual actor but to familiarize himself with meaning-patterns typical of the society he is studying. In any particular case his interpretation of an action will only be more or less probable, but the more familiar he is with a given society, social type, or individual, the more likely his interpretation is to be correct. As an example, consider the case of the man who removes his hat from his head as he enters a church. In practically every case he will be doing so because this is a mark of respect, a socially sanctioned action appropriate to the case. But there is always the chance that some other explanation would be correct, such as that his head was itching and he wanted to scratch it. Clearly such questions play a great part in the determination of guilt in criminal law, where in most cases a subjective guilty intent, *mens rea*, must be established, as the admirable phrase goes 'beyond all reasonable doubt'.

Schutz's analysis establishes the independence of social scientific interpretation from any theory of psychic empathy. It anchors the explanation of social action firmly in the intersubjective, and therefore publicly available, patterns of thinking and acting of the life-world, but this does not complete the picture. Though we can now explain individual actions, on a balance of probabilities, by reference to established meaning-patterns within society, we have not yet explained the meaning-patterns themselves. Meaning, I emphasize again, is not established in an existential vacuum. Meaning-patterns, whether scientific theories, religious doctrines, moralities, philosophies or myths, are not arbitrary creations but articulate responses to the problems of man's being in the world, related not only to each other but also to a physical and imperfectly known context which none can ignore or define away without rendering its own 'truth' implausible. The cognitive horizon of the unquestioning inhabitant of society is normally formed by the socially approved symbols, ideas and values of his native place, but these have their own cosmological context. As Gregor Sebba wrote of Voegelin's turn from the perspective of the history of political ideas to what was to become the root insight of *Order and History*, [18] Voegelin realized in the course of study that 'The ideas were not "ideas" — speculations about political society, or more or less arbitrary inventions of gifted thinkers, or rationalizations of emotional attitudes and vested interests. They were part of something much larger: of an ongoing process of symbolization extending over the whole realm of human expression and interpretation as we encounter it in the very form of political society, in the order of religion, in the world of thought and art.'[19] The terms 'human expression' and 'interpretation' refer respectively to what I have called, following Vivas, the elements of creation and discovery present in every human endeavour to come to terms with reality. Symbols, ideas and values arise historically as attempts to answer questions that man faces as a certain sort of being in a certain sort of world. And these questions, though historical in the sense that they arise at a certain point in the journey of mankind, are essentially suprahistorical because they refer to fundamental defining elements of human and extra-human nature that are neither created nor changed by the events of history. Properly understood, then, these are ontological questions which, once clearly posed, define the limits of both sociological and historical interpretation. Here the task of interpretative sociology ends and that of fundamental ontology begins, but here too is the baseline of whatever truth social science may contain.

3 On Interpretation

I said in the previous chapter: 'In the last analysis . . . *verstehen*, as a method, refers back to the ontological clarification of the being of the actor in the world.' That is a particular, careful way of formulating the most basic point of my argument so far: that concern with the status of interpretative sociology leads us directly to questions of ontology. This is only a special case of the general truth that all efforts to understand reality, even when positivistically stated as questions of fact, involve, at least tacitly, speculative philosophical issues. I take this to be a function of the following characteristics of experienced reality and the place of positive human knowledge within it:

1 That the world of facts is not self-explanatory;
2 That facts, as a term covering individual items of experienced reality, only make sense when referred to other items of experience;
3 That, at the limit, this will always involve reference to what Schutz calls the transcendent infinity of time and space;
4 That these transcendencies outbound even potential experience;
5 That concern with the trans-experiential realm of transcendencies is integral to the human attempt to make sense of the world or find meaning in existence;
6 That this realm is open to speculation at more or less differentiated levels which we may provisionally designate symbol, myth and theory;
7 That such speculation is not arbitrary, being suggested in outline by the character of the experienced reality out of which sense must be made.

In part these points state formal conclusions to earlier arguments: in part they anticipate themes of this and later chapters. At the least they state an epistemological position that depends on a realistic recognition of the constitutive limitations of man's peculiar position in the surrounding universe.

In so far as social reality is a humanly constituted realm of meaning, sociology, as a generic name for the disciplines which study that realm, may be called a hermeneutic discipline, a science that understands man through the interpretation of human expressions. But where this hermeneutic science uncovers constancies in the human condition, interpretation gives way to explanation. The relationship between interpretation and explanation is the theme of a later chapter; for the moment let us say that social reality, in all its diversity, is delimited in its possibilities and thus, in a fundamental sense, explained by the character of these constancies. Beneath the diversity of cultural expressions lie the ontological constants of man's being in the world. Analysis of these expressions, as Jonas shows, reveals the perennial characteristics of human existence as they disclose the nature of man and his relationship to all about him. In the absence of direct empathy and before the creative range of human cultural achievement, interpretation of human expressions (hermeneutics in the broad sense) is the path the human sciences must follow if they are to grasp the constants of the human condition, the factors that ultimately explain the character of social reality. As Eliade writes: 'Even if we wanted to, we couldn't give up hermeneutics because we are the result of a millennial hermeneutical effort. Ultimately, we are the result of interpretations and reinterpretations of life, death, consciousness, creativity, etc, elaborated since the pre-Socratics, and even before (since the discovery of agriculture and metallurgy for example).'[1]

Beneath diversity lies unity, the unity of a common humanity which grounds all cultural expression. The grounding unity of cultural expressions, which is the *sine qua non* for their interpretation, is simultaneously a function of Man who expresses and his context which is indicated. In the context of any individual is included the reality of other human beings and thus, more precisely, while Man expresses, human nature is also an integral part of what is indicated. Man is a being within being and thus the grounding unity of cultural expressions, discernible beneath their diversity, can be seen as merely an aspect of a more fundamental unity of being. Man and all he does is part of a reality which coheres. That is why questions of epistemology must be secondary to those of ontology, and why the epistemological obsession characteristic of methodological debates in the human sciences should be displaced by a concern with ontology. The constancies of the human condition are identifiable at both the biological and the cultural level, but, as constancies, they are ontological, truths about being as such and man as a being within being. However, our knowledge of these constancies, though presumed in common sense and pre-supposed in almost everything we say, is, for science, not immediate. It is mediated through analysis and interpretation of natural and social reality. To find the ontological constants one must dig for them, and even sensitivity to what one is looking for may, when too selective, lead to a distortion of understanding, as in the case of the materialist who assumes that the physical need for food must lie at the source of every other activity. We are on the wrong path the moment we assume that any one of the constants, however vital, whether physical or cultural, has undisputed primacy over the others. Man is man, and endowed with the full range of potential, creative, human responses, as far back as we can trace him, and the fact that a particular potentiality is not actualized under certain conditions does not prove that it is absent. Failure to recognize this not only leads to dogmatic nonsense about the one all important factor that 'explains' or determines the course of human history, but also gives rise to such errors as Lucien Lévy-Bruhl's belief in the existence of a specific primitive mentality essentially different from that of modern Western man.

These considerations are important for our discussion of interpretation. They mean that problems of interpretation are essentially similar, whether we seek to understand a near neighbour or an archaic society remote in time and space. And this, in turn, allows us to proceed confidently in the attempt to interpret the symbolic expressions of such a society in terms of the highly differentiated vocabulary of philosophical and social scientific theory. The epistemological consequence of the ontological constancies is the possibility of translating utterances from one sign system to another. At the same time it is true that the relationship of symbol and myth to theory presents peculiar difficulties to the would-be interpreter. Plato first posed the problem of equivalence between myth and theory which will occupy us in the next chapter, but during the last hundred years or so a new urgency has entered the field. Several factors have conspired to force the problem of interpretation to the forefront of interest, and these factors are not merely results of intellectual problems connected with the theory of knowledge.

In the first place, over the last century Western man has been confronted with a mass of human data that demands interpretation. The discoveries of explorers and archaeologists alike have brought him face to face with the evidence and testimony of human existence lived in accord once with beliefs and assumptions profoundly different from his own. But this is not in itself the nub of the problem. Most societies have been aware of the existence of others whose way of life appeared strange and even repulsive, but the usual reaction has been one of dismissal or curiosity. Did not the Greeks invent the term 'barbarian' to describe those outside the Hellenic orbit? Our language preserved precisely the most unfavourable connotations of the word. The usual assumption the man of one culture makes when confronted with another has been that it is self-evidently right to judge the other by the standards prevailing in his own community. Until recently this has also been the attitude of the West. 'Christians are right and pagans wrong,' says *The Song of Roland,* and even after the decline of the spiritual confidence and homogeneity of Christendom, Western man still found evidence of his superiority in his technical achievements sufficient to dismiss the achievement of 'savages' as existentially unimportant even when historically interesting. This is the particular blindness of the nineteenth-century cult of progress, a classic example of which is provided by Auguste Comte's law of three stages.

According to Comte, the human mind advances through the theological and metaphysical stages in order to arrive at the positive stage of modern scientific thinking. This third stage is seen as involving the abandonment of all theological and metaphysical questions of ultimate realities and first causes, in favour of a single-minded concern with the charting of regular connections between observable facts.

The experience of the twentieth century has shown up the narrowness of this attitude. Political history since 1914 shows that we ought no longer to confuse technical with ethical progress, for how, on a single scale of progress covering both technology and morality, can we place the Zyklon B gas chamber or the neutron bomb? Also, the defects of the positivist conception of science, which found its main support in the belief that Newtonian physics marked a final definitive insight into the structure of the universe, are now only too apparent. Einstein's formulation of the theory of relativity has among other things made the term 'speculation' respectable once again. We can now see clearly that while the observational study of facts provides a measure for the validity of theoretical speculation, it cannot ever replace it. This makes us more appreciative of the speculative genius of other civilizations, especially when we realize how such speculations are governed by the desire to make sense of the same universe which provided Newton and Einstein with their problems. This is not to claim that all speculative languages or systems are of equal cognitive value. We may be proud of the way Western scientific and philosophical language has developed a vocabulary sufficiently differentiated to permit the formulation of different kinds of problems in different ways. This is something that cannot really be said for the language of myth which, for instance, typically confuses the level of ethics with that of physics as where illness is conceived in terms of a punishment for moral fault. But the superiority of our conceptual vocabulary justifies only our continued use and development of its resources in order to make the distinctions necessary to the investigation of reality: it does not permit us to dismiss as unreal the problems and mysteries out of which myth makes sense. Indeed, though we can see scientific progress in terms of the gradual disengagement of certain types of problem from the sphere of myth and their appropriation by the empirical sciences of the external world, the inherent transcendencies of experience dictate that this disengagement will never be complete. The mystery of the beginning and the beyond, the living source of symbol and myth, is less mortal than man who finds in it his ultimate cognitive horizon.

In our largely literate and desacralized civilization, patterns of meaning, the rules of behaviour and thinking by which we introduce order and sense into our lives, generally take a relatively rational discursive form; but faced with the evidence of man's history we must recognize that the range of human articulation of meaning is much wider than contemporary Western experience would suggest. The very use of the term 'desacralized' draws our attention to the fact that until recently Western man understood his political institutions to be meaningful vehicles of participation in the transcendent reality of the cosmos. The social order, conceived symbolically as simultaneously *microcosmos*, the earthly analogue of cosmic order, and *macroanthropos*, man writ large, is still probably sufficiently a residual part of our conception of existence to allow us to understand how a similar experience has shaped and supported the lives of men throughout the ages. As Voegelin writes:

> Human society is not merely a fact, or an event, in the external world to be studied by an observer like a natural phenomenon. Though it has externality as one of its important components, it is as a whole a little world, a cosmion, illuminated with meaning from within by the human beings who continuously create and bear it as the mode and condition of their self-realization. It is illuminated through an elaborate symbolism, in various degrees of compactness and differentiation — from rite, through myth, to theory — and this symbolism illuminates it with meaning in so far as the symbols make the internal structure of such a cosmion, the relations between its members and groups of members, as well as its existence as a whole, transparent for the mystery of human existence.[2]

Voegelin's observations point up the necessary connection between the content of meaning patterns as immanent to a society, and the wider human requirement that such patterns make sense of the pre-given nature of human existence in the world. This requirement covers social and political institutions as much as the most obviously sense-endowing area of religious, philosophical and scientific discourse. For instance, there would be no institution of marriage without the duality of the sexes which we share with all higher animals; yet, as an institution, a marriage cannot be said to succeed if it is experienced as an imposed curb upon the sexual drive. Social institutions, no less than doctrines or beliefs, have a symbolic dimension. They function as external constraints upon the freedom of the individual but also as the modes through which the individual inhabitant orders his participation in the wider order of reality. Where this ceases to be true, where the symbolic function is obscured, as when the social order is conceived in purely instrumental individual terms, the institutional framework becomes a brittle shell, resented and despised. Where a political order ceases to evoke meaningful participation and its component institutions are no longer perceived as mediating between the individual and the cosmos or its history, social existence is degraded to the level of resentful conformity with rules that seem utterly unintelligible. Where that happens a political order will not long survive unless it is periodically reimposed by brute force, as happens when a nation defeated in war is subjected to foreign occupation.

The requirement of meaningful participation has no necessary connection with the existence of Western style formal representative institutions. Outside the ideological framework of liberalism there is nothing paradoxical in the notion of a 'participatory autocracy'. The reality of participation has much more to do with a sense of belonging, a being-part-of something greater than oneself, than with the demand for wider involvement in decision making. One thing the political history of this century has demonstrated in Europe between the wars and in Asia and Africa since decolonization, is that it is one thing to give people the formal institutions of representative democracy, and quite another for them to experience them as the proper or satisfactory framework for social life. Indeed, even in established liberal democracies people who are left cold by the formally essential business of making a choice among candidates in national or local elections experience a real sense of participation in mass meetings of the party faithful.

We may say, then, that man in society articulates his participation in reality in symbolic forms that range in type from political institutions to religious rituals and doctrines. Each answers a need or a question of human existence and, as such, the character of each can never be a matter of definition without reference to the character of existence as it is given to experience. The nature of the extra-human real demands recognition. There are, as Schutz says, universal forces which govern cosmos, individual and community alike, which man must 'conjure' or 'appease', for he does not create or constitute them and he cannot dominate them. The sense-endowing efficacy of symbols is directed to this realm. It is to the dependency of his mental and material works upon what we must call the order of Being that the symbolic imperative refers. Man creates symbols and reads cognitive significance into his creations because, whether justified or not in his belief, he will not accept that he is no more than a cosmic accident. At the very least, we can say that man searches for meaning in his existence and that the world permits possible meaning to be found. This tells us something of the subject who seeks meaning and of the object in which it is found. Social institutions and human actions must be interpreted not only in terms of their immanent structure but also in terms of what they say of the being who articulates himself through them and the world in which this takes place. Here is the source of the analogy between the interpretation of texts, hermeneutics in the strict sense, and the understanding appropriate to human action which Ricoeur, following and differing from the earlier suggestions of Dilthey, has developed in his recent work, and which will occupy us for the rest of this chapter.[3]

Whatever our verdict on Ricoeur's claim for the exemplary status of textual interpretation in the human sciences, and there are good reasons for considering it a particularly well explored and methodologically advanced area of the human sciences, the analogy itself is illuminating. Let us consider the different levels on which a text can be analysed. On the one hand it can be treated as an immanently structured system of signs closed in upon itself. This is the level of linguistic analysis and it has the effect, as Ricoeur puts it, of treating language as an absolute, a closed system of purely intrasignificative units. But if we treat a text in this way only we ignore the most important fact about language, which is that it speaks, in the sense that linguistic signs stand for something beyond language. 'Spoken words' as Aristotle says, 'are the symbols of mental experience and written words are the symbols of spoken words. Just as all men do not have the same writing, so all men do not have the same speech sounds, but the mental experiences, which these directly symbolize, are the same for all, as also are those things of which our experiences are the images.' A language is not only an immanently structured whole but evokes a reality which is beyond itself. The interpretation of language as a closed system of signs, necessary for the analytical purposes of linguistics, cannot be considered a substitute for a philosophy of language because it 'repudiates the basic intention of a sign, which is to hold "for", thus transcending itself and suppressing itself in what it intends. Language . . . as a signifying milieu, must be referred to existence.'[4] Hermeneutics treats language precisely in so far as it is significative of extra-linguistic reality. 'In hermeneutics', Ricoeur writes, 'there is no closed system of the universe of signs. While linguistics moves inside the enclosure of a self-sufficient universe of signs and encounters only intrasignificant relations . . . hermeneutics is ruled by the open state of the universe of signs. . . . In each hermeneutic discipline, interpretation is at the hinge between linguistics and non-linguistics, between language and lived experience.'[5]

To pursue this matter, I shall look more closely at Ricoeur's essay 'The Model of the Test: Meaningful Action considered as a Test'.[6] First the question arises why should we regard as especially important the techniques of textual interpretation in our search for an adequate conception of the nature of interpretation in the human sciences? It may appear that this priority is largely the result of historical accident, the fruit of nineteenth century historicism and the romantic interest in the exotic, the bizarre and the remote, an interest which gave rise to intense methodological debate among philosophers like Dilthey who sought to bring to consciousness the assumptions on which romantic procedures were based and to give them a more scientific character. Certainly, this is the immediate background of the long intellectual struggle to give an acceptable scientific content to the notion of empathy, but there is more to the matter than that. The science of textual interpretation has a longer history than is suggested by those accounts that start with the nineteenth century. Behind the broadening of hermeneutics in the last century lie the ages of disciplined Biblical exegesis and Classical philology, and in those fields, cultivated because of the cultural importance which their subjects possessed for European civilization, developed the central insight into the ontological distinctiveness of the written text as the most fixed or achieved form of human expression.

Biblical exegesis goes back at least as far as the first century Alexandrian Jewish writer Philo, who interprets scripture allegorically in a way compatible with the teachings of Greek philosophy. Philo was the first in a long line of exegetes and theologians, Jewish, Christian and Muslim, who established a substantial identity between the human content of the two traditions. Allegorical interpretation was only one of the ways, and not the most interesting, in which this could be carried out. Theologians of the Middle Ages were aware of the different levels of meaning present in the Bible and hence of the need for careful scholarship in interpretation. Even the leaders of the Reformation, who are sometimes portrayed as reacting against the complexities of interpretation by returning to the Biblical text itself, were aware that what they offered was not a transparent reading of a univocal text but another interpretation, whose claim to greater truth depended upon faithfulness to the original terms more than upon conformity to ecclesiastical tradition. The objection to Catholic tradition as mediating between the believer and the Bible was an objection to a particular procedure which made ecclesiastical mediation inevitable rather than to interpretation as such. Except among certain extreme sects, the Reformation demand for a return to 'pure' Biblical teaching did not involve any commitment to the view that the Bible is a God-given text no more or less than literally true at the surface level of its terms; and it is misleading to picture Protestant or Catholic theologians of the time as spiritual ancestors of such modern literalists as the Jehovah's Witnesses.

In biblical exegesis broad questions of meaning were primary and, apart from the particular problems of those who translated the scriptures into the various European vernaculars, the question of the accuracy of the text was secondary until the researches of the eighteenth and nineteenth centuries began to reveal the way in which the body of Holy Scripture had been put together by more hands and over a longer period than had ever been believed. But in the interpretation of classical texts, whose intellectual lucidity seemed often to preclude the question of levels of meaning, philological matters were always intensely debated. Especially after the fall of Constantinople precipitated a dispersal of Greek scholars and classical manuscripts throughout the Christian West, questions of accuracy and authenticity in the study of Classical literature became a central concern of the higher levels of an educational system centred on the study of the Classics.

The rise of hermeneutics in the nineteenth century can be seen as a combination of the interests of Biblical and Classical scholars extended to cover the whole range of written texts. Dilthey was the culmination of this development, and what he says of the significance of textual interpretation for the human sciences is relevant to our theme.

Because it is in language alone that human inwardness finds its complete, exhaustively and objectively comprehensible expression, literature is immeasurably significant for our understanding of intellectual life and history. The art of understanding therefore centres on the *interpretation of written records of human existence*. Therefore, the exegesis — and the critical treatment inseparably linked with it — of these records formed the starting-point of philology. This is essentially a personal skill and virtuosity in the treatment of written records; any interpretation of monuments or historically transmitted actions can only flourish in relation to this skill and its products. We can make mistakes about the motives of historical agents, indeed these agents may themselves mislead us about their motives; but the work of a great poet or explorer, of a religious genius or genuine philosopher, can only be the true expression of his mental life; in human society, full of lies, such work is always true and can therefore — in contrast to other permanent expressions — be interpreted with complete objectivity. Indeed it throws light on the other artistic records of an age and on the historic actions of contemporaries.[7]

Dilthey regarded the terms exegesis and interpretation as synonymous, because of the inevitable critical component in understanding, and defined hermeneutics as 'the methodology of the interpretation of written records.'[8]

The fact that Dilthey allows primacy in this field to the 'interpretation of written records of human existence' shows the extent to which, by 1900 when the passage was published, he recognized the mediated character of the understanding of the other, in contrast to the emphasis on empathy in his earlier work. 'By their works ye shall know them' is already in the later Dilthey the key motto of the theory of understanding. But for him the theory is still bound up with the historical idealist view of social reality as a manifestation of the activity of the human spirit. If all human discourse is potentially comprehensible both as expressive of man and significative of the surrounding reality of the world, it is primarily to the former pole that Dilthey refers his own theory. 'By understanding', he writes, 'I mean the process in which we use expressions given to the senses to gain knowledge of mental life.'[9]

Such a formulation is not wrong, but it is incomplete and the area in which it is incomplete emerges clearly in other passages from the draft manuscripts of 'The Development of Hermeneutics', where he writes, 'The possibility of apprehending something alien is one of the most difficult problems of epistemology. How can an individual understand another person's expressions objectively and validly? It is possibly only on the condition that the other person's expression contains nothing which is not also part of the observer. The same functions and elements are present in all individuals and their degree of strength accounts for the variety in the make-up of different people. The same external world is mirrored in every one's ideas . . .' This last, all-important, point is not developed, and in fact the point in the manuscript at which Dilthey introduces it is succeeded by two incomplete sentences, after which he returns to his treatment of the understanding of a work by reference to its author rather than to the world it evokes. Yet, once introduced, what I would call the objective dimension of understanding, the understanding of a text in terms of the world of which it speaks rather than the intentions of its author, is not easily banished, and soon we find him writing,

'Even particular mental states can only be understood in terms of the external stimulations which produced them. I can understand hatred in terms of the injury to life which caused it. Without this relationship I could have no idea of the passions. The environment is indispensable for understanding, which, at its most extreme, is indistinguishable from explanation (as far as we can explain mental states). Explanation, in turn, presupposes complete understanding.'[10]

Thus, having treated understanding as mediated knowledge of mental states, and identified 'complete understanding' as both indistinguishable from explanation and its precondition (a confusing statement to say the least), Dilthey admits the dependence of mental states upon the 'external world' and the stimulations it offers. All the elements are present for the solution of the problem but no solution is offered because certain distinctions have not been made. The development of these distinctions by such thinkers as Husserl, Schutz and Ricoeur shows us how the responsibility for his ultimate failure to solve the problem of interpretation rests on a typically Kantian confusion of epistemological and ontological issues. The distinctions I have in mind are Husserl's between the noetic and noematic aspects of consciousness, Schutz's between action and accomplished act, and Ricoeur's between spoken language and written text.

According to Husserl, consciousness is intentional: that is to say, all consciousness is consciousness-of some mental object. An act of consciousness that has no object is strictly inconceivable. Though Husserl's own teachings on the ontological status of the mental object, an issue he tried long to avoid, lead him in the direction of a transcendental idealism, the distinction that he draws between the act of consciousness, *noesis*, and the object of consciousness, *noema*, is the vital one, for the object of thought, or of love, or fear, is not produced by the act that recognizes it. By distinguishing so clearly what is thought from the act of thinking, Husserl adequately allows for the autonomous character of the object. And though Husserl's philosophy is ultimately idealist, in contrast to every other species of idealism it builds into itself, by the noesis/noema distinction, the realist recognition that what we think about is what it is regardless of whether we think about it or not. The essence of thought as act is the only essence that resides in the act of thinking *per se;* all others are part of a cognitive context to be discovered and not projected. The essence of reality is found in the object of thought and not in the act of thinking.

Schutz's distinction between action and accomplished act is similar to this. He thought that Weber had confused the theory of interpretative sociology by failing to distinguish between these two meanings of the term 'action'. If by action we intend meaningful behaviour as it is taking place, its meaning will be primarily known by reference to the subjective intentions of the actor; but if we mean the completed act, the meaning can be known by reference to the public intersubjective system of meaning-patterns operative in society. In contrast to an action in process the meaning of an accomplished act is understood by reference to the locus of its achievement, to its cultural, social and natural environment more than to the intentions of the actor. Indeed, when we say that an action has taken place, we indicate that its results have taken a place in the order of social reality and its significance is judged in accordance with the system of meanings that operate there. By the mediation of our knowledge of the public environment we approach knowledge of private, subjective intentions. This theory of understanding, as we have seen, points us in the direction of ontology and away from the necessarily obscure psychology of individual consciousness.

With Ricoeur's distinction between spoken language and written text we return to an area considered by Dilthey himself. Dilthey allows, like Ricoeur, primacy to the interpretation of written texts in his theory of understanding, but for rather different reasons. For Dilthey, 'The art of understanding . . . centres on the interpretation of written records . . .' because, 'in language alone human inwardness finds its complete, exhaustively and objectively comprehensible expression.' In other words, the privileged status of the text rests on its being a uniquely valuable clue to the secrets of the consciousness that stands behind it. Interpretation, for Dilthey, seeks a disclosure that is psychological and not ontological: it focuses on the mind behind the text and not on the world before it. For Ricoeur, in contrast, who specifically draws upon Husserl's noesis/noema distinction, the meaning of a text, its intentionality and depth semantics, is something other than the subjective intent, even in a psychoanalytic sense the unconscious intent, of the author. In dialogue, to ask the meaning of something said is usually to ask that the other clarify what he intended to convey; but with the written text, where the author is absent, clarification in this sense is not possible. This is not really the limitation to understanding which it may at first seem, for what discourse is about, what it conveys or evokes, is wider than the subjective intent of the writer. Indeed, even in dialogue, when we ask someone what he means we cannot depend on the truth of the clarification we obtain. Who has not retrospectively altered the intention, at least as he admits to it, of something he has said when he has realized the extent to which it wounds or gives offence?

Ricoeur's approach to the theory of understanding embodies the truth that, when we ask what something means, we are usually asking a question of a spoken or written expression whose terms embody meanings and references that precede and are wider than the intentions of the speaker or author.

> The depth-semantics of the text is not what the author intended to say but what the text is about, i.e., the non-ostensive reference of the text. And the non-ostensive reference of the text is the kind of world opened up by the depth-semantics of the text. Therefore what we want to understand is not something hidden behind the text, but something disclosed in front of it. What has to be understood is not the initial situation of discourse but what points toward a possible world. Understanding has less than ever to do with the author and his situation. It wants to grasp the world-propositions opened up by the references of the text. To understand a text is to follow its movements from sense to reference, from what it says to what it talks about . . . To understand an author better than he could understand himself is to display the power of disclosure implied in his discourse beyond the limited horizon of his own existential situation.[11]

Following Ricoeur, we can say that the status of the text is characterized by four traits which together constitute its peculiar objectivity. These are

1 The fixation of meaning;
2 Its dissociation from the mental intention of the author;
3 The display of non-ostensive references;
4 The universal range of its addresses.

Here we seek neither to reproduce the argument by which Ricoeur establishes this characterization, nor to examine the way in which he argues from it toward a particular view of the relationship between interpretation and explanation. The former is not directly relevant to our present interest in the parallel between textual interpretation and the procedures of interpretative sociology, and the latter will be considered when we turn specifically to the nature of the interpretation/explanation relationship. I shall refer only to those passages of Ricoeur's essay where he establishes the parallels between the specific features of the text and those of social action.

The first of these parallels lies in what he calls the 'fixation of action'. 'Meaningful action', he writes, 'is an object for science only under the condition of a kind of objectification which is equivalent to the fixation of discourse by writing.'[12] What is fixed by writing is what Ricoeur designates 'the *noema* of speaking', what is said and not the speech act itself. 'Like the speech-act, the action event . . . develops a similar dialectic between its temporal status as an appearing and disappearing event, and its logical status as having such-and-such identifiable meaning or "sense-content." '[13] Ricoeur argues that this fixation of the meaning of discourse in writing finds a parallel in the way such-and-such an event, or accomplished act, leaves its mark on its time. In being achieved, an action becomes an act, an event in time, that has an irredeemable significance for all that is about it and follows it. The application of the other three criteria of the text to action helps to make our understanding of the nature of this fixation more precise.

What Ricoeur calls the autonomization of action corresponds to the dissociation of the meaning of the text from the intentions of the author. 'In the same way that a text is detached from its author, an action is detached from its agent and develops consequences of its own. This autonomization of human action constitutes the *social* dimension of action. An action is a social phenomenon not only because it is done by several agents in such a way that the role of each of them cannot be distinguished from the role of others, but also because our deeds escape us and have effects which we did not intend.'[14] Actions, to speak metaphorically, make an imprint on their time, and time, in this sense, signifies 'social time', not merely a temporal flow but a 'place of durable effects, or persisting patterns. An action leaves a "trace", it makes its "mark" when it contributes to the emergence of such patterns which become the *documents* of human action.' To the record of human action we give the name of history, or, in Ricoeur's striking formulation:

> History is this quasi-'thing' *on* which human action leaves a 'trace', puts its mark. Hence the possibility of 'archives'. Before the archives which are intentionally written down by the memorialists, there is the continuous process of 'recording' human action which is history itself as the sum of 'marks', the fate of which escapes the control of individual actors. Henceforth history may appear as an autonomous entity, as a play with players who do not know the plot. This hypostasis of history may be denounced as a fallacy, but this fallacy is well entrenched in the process by which human action becomes social action when written down in the archives of history. Thanks to this sedimentation in social time, human deeds become 'institutions' in the sense that their meaning no longer coincides with the logical intentions of the actors. The meaning may be 'depsychologized' to the point where the *meaning* resides in the work itself.[15]

In action the parallel to the way a text 'breaks the ties of discourse to all the ostensive references' is found in the manner in which the significance of an action shows itself to be other than its relevance to its initial situation. 'As a result of this emancipation from the situational context, discourse can develop non-ostensive references which we called a "world", in the sense of which we speak of the Greek "world", not in the cosmological sense of the word, but as an ontological dimension.' Correspondingly,

> An important action . . . develops meanings which can be actualized or fulfilled in situations other than the one in which the action occurred. To say the same thing in different words, the meaning of an important event exceeds, overcomes, transcends the social conditions of its production and may be reenacted in new social contexts. Its importance is its durable relevance, and, in some cases, its omni-temporal relevance.[16]

Finally, like a text, a human action may be conceived as an 'open work',

> the meaning of which is 'in suspense'. . . . It is because it 'opens up' new references and receives fresh relevance from them, that human deeds are also waiting for fresh interpretations which decide their meaning. . . . Human action . . . is opened to anybody who *can read*. In the same way that the meaning of an event is the sense of its forthcoming interpretations, the interpretation by the contemporaries has no special privilege in this process.[17]

The methodological implications of this elaborate parallel are relatively simple. Indeed, the whole notion of a parallel between different objects may seem laboured given that a text is not something ontologically distinct from an accomplished human act but rather a particular type of achieved project, whose specificity lies in the material form in which the achievement is preserved. Either way, what is implied is the substantive identity of procedure between the practices of the various human sciences. Every action is, like a text, a limited field open to various interpretations, and Ricoeur, like Dilthey and like Karl Popper to whom he refers in this context, freely admits the element of personal skill or luck involved in the initial stages of understanding. All three, working from different perspectives, draw a distinction between the initial hypothesis, or guess, whose fruitfulness depends on such incalculable factors, and the scientific procedures by which hypotheses are tested and validated. Validation, Ricoeur admits, is necessarily probabilistic and provisional. It does not amount to verification on the positivist model. Nor does it involve a collapse into relativism. We may not prove the ultimate correctness of an interpretation but we can give good reasons for preferring one to another, just as, in a court of law, consideration of surrounding circumstances will lead a judge and jury to accept one story rather than another.

The linguistic and hermeneutic levels of analysis and interpretation of the written text provide potential models throughout the human sciences, precisely because every human expression not only possesses an inherent structure but refers to a reality beyond itself. Herein lies the clue to the solution of the problem noted in connection with the ideas of Winch and Phillipson. Approaches such as theirs, which treat meaning as something constituted and maintained by a self-referent system of social conventions, correspond, no less than more obvious structuralist theories like those of Lévi-Strauss, to the level of linguistics, which treats language as an immanently structured system of signs closed in on itself. While the hermeneutic level is represented by an interpretative sociology which takes account of the universal ontological reference of human expressions.

The fact that it is possible to 'read' and understand a social or political institution as expressing a certain sort of being and indicating the place of that being in reality, provides the social sciences with a way out of that relativist maze which overwhelms many social scientists who take the humanly constituted dimensions of social reality with the seriousness they deserve. This relativism is almost entirely the result of treating socially sanctioned meaning-systems in abstraction from ontological considerations. By reintroducing them we can judge between conflicting patterns of meaning — Western science and Azande witchcraft to take a favourite instance — by reference to the extent to which each discloses the potentialities of a world that all share. As in every case relating to aspects of experience, the determination of truth involves, more than coherence, an element of correspondence between the symbolic pattern and the character of the world. The difficulties philosophers have in formulating what we mean by correspondence are no warrant to ignore its requirement, for in contrast to the problem of empathy, with which the correspondence problem may seem to possess common features, both the elements we seek to bring into harmony, symbolic expression and experienced reality, exist in publicly available form as the content of a mind does not. That there is a shared world, constant in its characteristics and in the forms of creative response it evokes in man, is adequately shown by the arguments of Jonas cited in the last chapter. Its very existence gives us the assurance that subjectivism and relativism need not be the last words. Yet the fact remains that at present there is little sign of ontological awareness among most social scientists. They tend to react with suspicion to suggestions of ontological exigency in the forms of society beyond historical and volitional factors. The language of human nature and natural order, in the classical or scholastic sense, is scarcely fashionable in the modern sciences of man. Yet, as the study of social reality will make clear, it remains the most adequate vocabulary we possess in our attempt to know ourselves and the reality about us.

4 Symbol, Myth and Theory

Between social theory and its object, social reality, there is a certain inevitable tension. In the following pages I shall examine the nature and significance of this tension. Its underlying reasons are not hard to see. As Schutz points out, the interpretative constructs of the social sciences are constructs of the second degree; they are always attempts to make sense of, to extract communicable meaning from, a realm of reality that already possesses a sense structure for those who inhabit it. The interpretation of a social scientist is like the semantic clarification undertaken by the philosopher of language: it is directed toward a realm already formed by other human beings in their effort to discover a structure of meaning in existence. In Voegelin's terms the linguistic and institutional symbols that operate in social reality make transparent for the inhabitants the mystery of their existence. They are governed, I shall suggest, by the need to establish meaning in the world, and, as such, they claim both to make sense in themselves and to provide an account of surrounding reality that is true. Science and philosophy, too, aspire to speak truly about reality, but their criteria of truth are critical ones developed in the struggle to attain an ever clearer understanding of experienced reality in the face of a course of events that all too often threatens to shatter the framework of accepted meaning. What these criteria are I shall examine in the next chapter, but here it is enough to say that in so far as the truth-seeking sciences and philosophy take social reality for their object they touch upon an area which already makes its own claim to represent or embody truth, and this claim's adequacy the theorist is likely to question.

The analysis of ideology and myth are two areas where this tension is manifest. For instance, an analysis of political ideology that discovers particular and exclusive power relationships beneath such self-interpretative and self-affirming formulae as 'popular sovereignty' or 'majority rule' will inevitably challenge a political community that understands its own structure or purpose in terms of such symbols. The case is similar with myth. The 'explanation' of a myth, even the interpretation of its symbols in a language acceptable to Western logic and science, threatens its claim to recount a true story. As Ricoeur shows, even when the philosopher or human scientist recognizes a positive cognitive value in myths (or ideologies for that matter) it is not the same value they have for those who accept them as accounts of a succession of peculiarly significant events. An adequate modern philosophy of man can, indeed must, be informed by contact with the themes of myth, but, from its critical perspective, it is true to its vocation only in rejecting the explanatory and historical pretensions of the mythic tale. Myth retains for us its value as a mode of ontological exploration, an attempt to speak of that about which we should otherwise be forced to keep silence; for those who live by it, myth is something far more concrete.

Myths, for instance any of those myths that explain the origins of the universe, continue to point to the boundaries of understanding and cognitive possibility within which philosophy and the human sciences — unlike myth itself in so far as it 'narrates' and 'explains' — must operate. The critical self-awareness of philosophical and scientific theory involves a recognition that there are areas of reality that lie beyond the competence of positive knowledge. Theory reminds metaphorical discourse of its specific problematic relationship to reality. It recalls to myth the genius of symbolization, to bring to apparent knowledge that which is not in fact known at all, or at least not known as science knows its object. Voegelin wrote of the status of mythical symbols in a text sent to Schutz in 1943:

> A mythical symbol is a finite symbol supposed to provide 'transparence' for a transfinite process. Examples: A myth of creation, which renders transparent the problem of the beginning of a transfinite process of the world; an immaculate conception, which mediates the experience of a transfinite spiritual beginning; an anthropomorphic image of God, which finitizes an experience of transcendence; speculations about the pre-existence or post-existence of the soul, which provide a finite formula for the beyond of birth and death; the fall and original sin, which illuminate the mystery of finite existence through procreation and death; and son on.[1]

Thus experience is brought to meaningful expression, the ontological mysteries of beginning and beyond to a first level discourse that both illumines experience and clothes its naked terrors with meaning. A second level of discourse, theory, picks the fabric apart and distinguishes the elements of illumination and obfuscation tightly woven together in myth.

Because we can recognize the role of myth as ontological exploration to be more basic than its pretensions to provide explanations, philosophy and science, which originate in the rejection of mythical explanations couched in terms of a dramatic narrative, can still be informed by the human experience enshrined in the mythic culture of archaic societies. Theory challenges myth because its differentiated language distinguishes realms of being, actual and potential, human and superhuman, natural and ethical, held together in the compact expression of myth; but, as it challenges, it identifies the enduring mysteries that mythical thought evokes more clearly than myth itself.

Two motifs, one from Ricoeur, the other from Voegelin, throw light on my perspective. In *The Symbolism of Evil*, Ricoeur takes 'myth' to mean what the history of religions finds in it:

> not a false explanation by means of images and fables, but a tradi-
> tional narration that relates to events that happened at the beginning of
> time and which has the purpose of providing grounds for the ritual
> actions of men of today and, in a general manner, establishing all the
> forms of action and thought by which man understands himself in his
> world. For us, moderns, a myth is *only* a myth because we can no longer
> connect that time with the time of history as we write it, employing the
> critical method, nor can we connect mythical places with our
> geographical space. That is why myth can no longer be an explana-
> tion; to exclude its etiological intention is the theme of all necessary
> demythologization. But in losing its explanatory pretensions the
> myth reveals its exploratory significance and its contribution to under-
> standing, which we shall call its symbolic function — that is to say, its
> power of discovering and revealing the bond between man and what he
> considers sacred.[2]

From Voegelin we draw the theory of symbolization itself, which is a process entailed in both myth and theory. Voegelin's theory results from his dissatisfaction with Husserl's subject-centred theory of consciousness, and his effort, in debate with Schutz, to achieve an alternative theory, one which recognized the ontological dependence of consciousness upon surrounding reality of which consciousness is a part and in which it is an event.

> There is, wrote Voegelin in 1943, no absolute starting point for a
> philosophy of consciousness. All philosophizing about consciousness
> is an event in the consciousness of philosophizing and presupposes this
> consciousness itself with its structures. Inasmuch as the consciousness
> of philosophizing is no 'pure' consciousness but rather the conscious-
> ness of a human being, all philosophizing is an event in the philo-
> sopher's life history, further an event in the history of the community
> with its symbolic language; further in the history of mankind, and
> further in the history of the cosmos. No 'human' in his reflection on
> consciousness and its nature can make consciousness an 'object' over
> against him; the reflection rather is an orientation within the space of
> consciousness by which he can push to the limit of consciousness but
> never cross those limits. Consciousness is given in the elemental sense
> that the systematic reflection on consciousness is a late event in the bio-
> graphy of the philosopher. The philosopher always lives in the con-
> text of his own history, the history of a human existence in the commu-
> nity and in the world.[3]

Consciousness is a finite event in a transfinite process of reality. The limitation of knowledge by mystery flows from this for, as Voegelin wrote later, 'There is psyche deeper than consciousness, and there is reality deeper than reality experienced, but there is no consciousness deeper than consciousness.'[4] Thus, though the condition of man's existence is his partnership in transcendent reality, he never knows what the essential order of this reality may be:

> Knowledge of the whole . . . is precluded by the identity of the knower with the partner, and ignorance of the whole precludes essential knowledge of the part . . . (yet) ultimate, essential ignorance is not complete ignorance. Man can achieve considerable knowledge about the order of being, and not the least part of that knowledge is the distinction between the knowable and the unknowable. Such achievement, however, comes late in the long-drawn-out process of experience and symbolization. . . . The concern of man about the meaning of his existence in the field of being does not remain pent up in the tortures of anxiety, but can vent itself in the creation of symbols purporting to render intelligible the relations and tensions between the distinguishable terms of the field.[5]

The ability to make symbols, which is at the root of myth and theory alike, helps man to orient himself in the world in a way that has meaning for him. In their attempt to make sense of existence, men can develop ever more adequate symbols through reflective analysis provoked by the pressure of events, and in this process the symbols of theory represent a higher level of truth than those of myth. Theory makes distinctions between the known, the unknown and the unknowable that myth does not, and the truth claims of theory thus call into question the truth of all rival symbolic systems, whether of common sense, myth or ideology. Theory refines truth from the ore of experience, but the ore is already mined by the work of less differentiated levels of discourse. At those levels truth is already present but its outline not yet clearly seen. The symbols of theory are based in the secondary, reflective analysis of experience as already interpreted and expressed by more compact modes of discourse. The justification of theory lies in its power to illumine areas of existence that were shadowed before.

Inevitably theory is a challenge, and a truly theoretical sociology particularly so, to a society which exists, as all societies do, at a pre-theoretical level of self interpretation. Society is not a system of mechanical or merely external relations. Our participation in social life demands a cognitive involvement, a commitment to finding sense in what we do. That sense is embodied in socially approved pre-theoretical meaning-patterns. We proceed in habitual grooves of behaviour and thought which we take to be appropriate paths to our particular projects. And they often are. But in so far as shared meaning-patterns claim to represent truth (and which proverb, however trivial, does not make this majestic claim to some degree?) they seem, by the critical standards of theory, a hotch-potch. We may value them as supports for life, but for the theorist that will not be sufficient.

Among sociologists, Peter Berger is especially sensitive to the implications of this, and in the introduction to his essays *Facing up to Modernity*, he clarifies what they are. Sociology, he admits, is in one sense subversive of established patterns of thought, hence its appeal to political radicals. Yet at the same time, it is profoundly conservative in its implications for institutional order. It is subversive because its investigation brings to consciousness the roots of much that is normally taken for granted in social life. The pre-reflective conservatism of what Schutz called 'the world-taken-for-granted' which expresses itself in the conviction that 'that's the way things have to be' is implicitly questioned when the sometimes trivial historical reasons are brought to light. Social science questions the ontological necessity assumed in our pre-reflective acceptance of established meaning-patterns, customs and modes of behaviour.

But this is only half the story. Objectively the science of man will discover the defining limits of human existence and possibility, while subjectively we should not be gratified to see the cognitive precariousness of social order. 'Society in its essence,' writes Berger, 'is the imposition of order upon the flux of human experience,' and 'order is *the* primary imperative of social life.'[6] The taken-for-granted explanations, remedies and recipes of society make sense, however provisionally, of the mystery of being. They also, as Arnold Gehlen argues, lessen the burden of choice which would otherwise impose impossible tensions upon the mind. The tension between sociology and social reality, between analysis and established order, is a special case of the wider tension that exists between a discourse which pursues truth wherever that pursuit may lead, and one that rests content with the provisional comfort of established patterns of meaning. This tension is clearest in the relationship between myth and theory. Myth and theory are brothers. They spring from the same ground — man's capacity to orient himself in reality through the creation of symbols — yet their imperatives are crucially different. We can see this difference by examining the path taken by theoretical understanding and the circumstances in which the level of theory is most likely to be achieved. How and why, we ask, does a theory of man in society arise?

In social reality we confront a common-sense world intrinsically meaningful to its inhabitants. Within it meaning is articulated in a wide range of discursive forms, such as proverbs, moralities, political and religious beliefs, and also through an institutional system which is experienced by the inhabitants as a mode of participation in reality. Except at moments of crisis, institutions are an ordering framework for the life of the individual less because they exercise external constraint upon him than because they provide channels for activity that seem to make sense of life. Obviously these forms of meaning are human expressions, but they are not arbitrary. They are creative responses to the pressures of experience, and if we think of social science as engaged in the task of interpreting them we find that such interpretation will take the special form that Husserl called *rückfrage,* or back-questioning. To interpret a human expression is, fundamentally, to uncover its root in the historical and cosmological experience of men. For Husserl the notion of back-questioning leads to the level of transcendental subjectivity. For us, following Voegelin and Schutz, it leads to the ontic level of reality experienced as external to and independent of the individual, and the ontological experience of man as a partner in being.

In calling the constructs of the social sciences 'constructs of the second degree', Schutz draws attention to the specificity of social science as a level of interpretation whose object is already a tissue of meaning spun out of experience and laid upon it by a more or less spontaneous process of meaning establishment in the world. Within this tissue various elements are already present. They include primary symbols, mythologies and even apparent strands of theory. In his book on Ricoeur, Don Ihde describes his hermeneutics of symbols as characterized by the double relationship between experience and expression and between expression and interpretation.[7] This double relationship also describes accurately that between sociological theory and social reality, the constructs of the second and the first degree. An ontologically aware social science begins with the analysis of human expressions so that it may discover within them the basic contours of man's being in the world. It is remarkable how we may, within the infinite variety of human expressions, find constancies in experience to which these discursive and institutional symbolic expressions are creative responses.

Striking examples of this can be found in Eliade's *Patterns in Comparative Religion,* [8] in which he shows through the study of a vast number of religious myths a constant core of meaning in each of the primary symbols found throughout the religions of the world. Inevitably, it seems, men fix upon a certain species of symbol to express a certain sense of relationship to what surrounds them. Beyond historical accident and such factors as ethnic relationship and the influence of geographical proximity, there appears to be an equivalence between types of experience and certain primary symbols. The case is not very different in that other field of symbolic expression, man's articulation of his life in society in the creation of social and political institutions, though here the reasons for equivalence are easier to understand. A wide range of institutions, such as those governing the organization of patterns of dominance or the socialization of the young, can be seen to correspond to a relatively small number of basic types, and each type can, in turn, be understood to answer to a particular functional exigency for the survival of a human society. Basic types of institution, like primary symbols, can, in theory, be questioned for what they tell us of the human reality they evoke and of the cosmic-historical reality to which each is a creative reaction. In the class of basic symbols and in the limited range of institutions necessary to the existence of a society, we find evidence of a constancy, at once psychological, anthropological and cosmological in the nature of man's being in the world. It is at this point that phenomenological, functionalist and ontological interpretations of society transcend rivalry to combine in a general theory of man.

The meaningful character of social reality is articulated through a first-level interpretation of experienced reality, and this is governed both by the desire to survive, common to all animals, and by the specifically human need to find and express sense and order in experience. Theoretical understanding of this realm takes the form of back-questioning from social expression to the engendering human experience. However, such an activity depends not only upon a specific cognitive interest in carrying it out but upon a level of linguistic sophistication that permits the theorist to operate with some independence of established first-level meaning patterns. This is the origin of technical terms and unusual uses of every-day terms which causes resentment outside the scientific community. Certainly, there is abuse of this procedure, and jargon can be used to cover an emptiness of thought and content: yet, originally, the purpose of the special vocabularies developed by each science is to clarify and not to obscure. The difficulty such vocabularies cause 'laymen' is a function of their need to articulate real distinctions hidden at less differentiated levels of discourse.

We cannot question the truth of a myth, for instance, unless we have a language that does not lead us back to mythical explanations. Thus our language, and the experience which provokes its specifically theoretical development, must be sufficiently differentiated to allow us to distinguish a realm where dramatic narrative, the form of myth, is appropriate from one where it is not. An experience of the inadequacy of a believed myth to cope with experience usually attends on the birth of theory. The Greek philosophical account of origins could only be developed in opposition to cosmogonic myth because, parallel with the philosophers, the great Greek historians were distinguishing probable historical truth from popular legend. What is remarkable about the *History* of Herodotus is not only the vast store of myth and folklore it contains, but also the fact that its author goes out of his way to draw attention to the failure of such elements to conform to the critical criteria of historical science. This is the specific difference that sets the method of Herodotus and his successors apart from that of Homer.

Philosophy, like history and the other human sciences, develops only when men emerge sufficiently from the mythical universe of inclusive meaning to admit, 'we do not really know'. The achievement of the level of science depends on a recognition of the frontiers of nescience. To the rich dramatic narrative and inclusive meaning of myth, theory replies with the development of criteria of truth. Socrates' conception of true knowledge as knowledge that respects its limits is the archetype of all such distinction. His fate dramatically illustrates where the tension between theory and its human object may lead.

Peter Berger and Thomas Luckmann explore the composition of a meaningful world in *The Social Construction of Reality*. Man, they argue, is a being

> biologically predestined to construct and to inhabit a world with others. This world becomes for him the dominant and definite reality. Its limits are set by nature, but, once constructed, this world acts back upon nature. In the dialectic between nature and the socially constructed world the human organism itself is transformed. In this same dialectic man produces reality and thereby produces himself.[9]

There are three dialectical moments in social reality: 'Society is a human product. Society is an objective reality. Man is a social product.'[10] Men, in this view, make society, though always within natural limits which represent an ontological baseline, and society, 'the imposition of order upon the flux of human experience', then defines what will be recognized as reality. Certain patterns of human interaction are habitualized and thus institutions arise. These institutions come to be regarded as 'facts of life'. Once established and if challenged they are explained in more or less coherent terms; that is they are legitimized. 'The function of legitimation is to make objectively available and subjectively plausible the "first-order" objectivations that have been institutionalized.'[11]

Berger and Luckmann identify four levels of legitimation, each of which serves to structure the particular reality into which the new member of society (child or outsider) is socialized on the basis of a shared view of reality. The first level

> is present as soon as a system of linguistic objectifications of human experience is transmitted. For example, the transmission of a kinship vocabulary *ipso facto* legitimates the kinship structure. The fundamental legitimating 'explanations' are, so to speak, built into the vocabulary. Thus a child learns that another child *is* a cousin, a piece of information that immediately and inherently legitimates the conduct with regard to 'cousins' that is learned along with the designation.[12]

To name something is to say what it is, and to say what it is will, in each society, imply a certain behavioural orientation toward it. At the second level we find the most elementary theoretical propositions relating to concrete situations, and these include proverbs, maxims and legends. Beyond these is the third level encompassing explicit theories legitimating particular institutions. Examples include such theories as the divine right of kings and that of popular sovereignty which legitimates elective institutions.

The fourth level of legitimation, the ultimate framework of meaning-reference in social reality, consists in the grand constructions for which Berger and Luckmann reserve the name 'symbolic universes'. At this level we find cosmological theories that purport to make meaningful the nature of the universe and man's place within it. 'These are bodies of theoretical tradition that integrate different provinces of meaning and encompass the institutional order in a symbolic totality.'[13] Here, in Voegelin's terms, the transfinite process of reality is made transparent, or conceptualized in intelligible terms, by means of finite symbols. At this level things are so and not otherwise not because a relative tells us, nor even because there exist convincing theories justifying each thing in particular, but because that is how the nature of things, the universal character of reality, is apprehended. The modern alternatives to such cosmologies are the various historicist constructions that have grown up since the Enlightenment and which pretend to discover a 'law' governing the direction and end of the historical process. In such 'theories', as in ancient cosmologies, every event can be seen to have an objective place and meaning in the unfolding story.

Like the lower levels of legitimation, symbolic universes are social products, each with a history and a root in experience that are open to investigation. But characteristically these roots are not uncovered. We grow into acceptance of a framework of understanding as we are socialized into the society of which we are members. The symbolic universe is not only the ultimate point of reference for lower levels of legitimation: it gives meaning to each life by placing it in a comprehensible cosmos, a universe which we can understand and in which we can feel at home.

> The origins of a symbolic universe have their roots in the constitution of man. If man in society is a world constructor, this is made possible by his constitutionally given world-openness, which already implies the conflict between order and chaos. Human existence is, *ab initio,* an ongoing externalization. As man externalizes himself, he constructs the world *into* which he externalizes himself. In the process of externalization, he projects his meanings into reality. Symbolic universes which proclaim that *all* reality is humanly meaningful and call upon the *entire* cosmos to signify the validity of human existence, constitute the furthest reaches of this projection.[14]

Thus the child receives and the adult maintains the universe of his experience as a whole, an ordered stage for the drama of his life and death. Yet, as Berger and Luckmann recognize, every symbolic universe is precarious, precisely because each has objective reference to the level of immediate experience. Established meaning-patterns may make sense of the past but they cannot dictate the future nor allow for the challenges experience will bring to the inclusive meaning-patterns they claim to discover. Nevertheless a symbolic universe is a supple construction. Its conceptual apparatus can often encompass experiences which might at first seem to shatter its plausibility and subjectively destroy its validity. The history of the Israelites recounted in the Old Testament is in large part the story of the changing interpretations made by the Jews of the meaning of the Covenant between Yahweh and his people, under the pressure of historical events. Time and again the symbolism of the Covenant, which was formative for the consciousness of the Jewish people and alone made their existence as God's chosen meaningful, survived history's refutation of its earlier interpretations. The most interesting thing about this is not the anthropological fact of human attachment to inherited meaning-patterns, but the way in which the gravest of historical crises — for instance the fall of Jerusalem and the interruption of the Temple cult — can provoke reinterpretations that are later legitimately seen as cognitive advances. For the Israelites this advance took the form of a growing realization of the transcendence of God and the chasm that divides earthly political from Divine order. This development is the more extraordinary in the light of the continuing dominance of the symbolic analogy between cosmic and human order in the surrounding civilizations. In the history of Israel a tension in reality was brought to consciousness that had not been seen before.[15]

A symbolic universe is governed by the imperative of meaning-establishment in experience. Changes in it, provoked by the pressure of experience, are directed toward papering over the cracks in the fabric of meaning. But there can come a point at which the conscious attempt to make sense of reality breaks with this particular imperative: when the effort to re-establish consonance between meaning and experience leads to the attempt to state general criteria of truth; and when the application of these criteria to the interpretation of experienced reality leads to a fundamental break with the charmed universe of myth, in which everything is meaningful because everything can be 'explained' by reference to an originary tale.

This is something that happens in the history of consciousness. There is nothing determined about it. No cluster of events will cause it, but, retrospectively, we can recognize that certain circumstances make it more possible. These are situations of cognitive crisis in which established meaning-patterns of inclusive range, the 'symbolic universes', come to be seen, if only by one sufficiently articulate man, as irretrievably dissonant with experienced reality. Outside the genius of the exceptional seeker there is no sufficient cause for the birth of theory in the strict sense in which we will henceforth use the term; that is, as a symbolic system critically oriented toward truth rather than plausible meaning. A theoretical mind admits the possibility of ultimate meaninglessness as a mythical mind does not. History provides examples of symbolic universes which have broken down leaving a vacuum behind them. Particularly in the last few centuries of European expansion aboriginal peoples, especially in Australasia and the Americas, have seen the web of meaning in their lives destroyed by the encounter with the white man. In some cases breakdown has been so total that whole tribes have literally seemed to lose the will to survive. The listlessness and hopelessness of a reservation-bound tribe, cut off from its ancestral lands and the shrines of its gods, have sometimes betokened approaching extinction quite as much as the physical marks of smallpox or the plague.

In other cases the breakdown of a native system of meaning has been accompanied by the adoption of another, equally inclusive and more cognitively attuned to the new circumstances of life. The spread of Christianity and Islam in Africa is a striking example. The uncritical fideism of African Christianity in particular is evidence of a novelty of attachment between the believer and his faith, in which the meaning-system offered by the new religion has not yet been severely tested by experience. There is no condescension in saying this. A religion is *par excellence* an inclusive framework of meaning, and in the case of Christianity, though not Christianity alone, one which makes intelligible the relationship between the individual believer, the origins and Author of the Cosmos, and the destiny of the human soul after death. In drawing attention to the pre-critical character of belief among those new to Christianity, I intend to indicate that their faith has not yet passed through those crises of definition born of experiences which render Christian meaning problematic. To such experiences we owe the extraordinary theological richness of European Christianity. This is recognized implicitly in the Catholic view of tradition, which embodies the Church's awareness that in time even a revealed truth may come to be understood more deeply through reflection on its content in the context of shifting history.

The doctrine of tradition is only a formal legitimation for that cognitive dynamism exemplified in the periodic reinterpretation of the meaning of the Covenant between God and Israel. This is how the great religions, in contrast to literalist sects, transcend the level of myth in the direction of the critical theoretical pursuit of truth. Nevertheless, inasmuch as a religion remains an inclusive meaning-system aspiring to encompass all being, it must retain what are, from the standpoint of theory, mythical elements in its positive account of what is beyond the reach of positive knowledge. Theory, or rather that theory which does not operate within a pre-theoretical acceptance of special revelation, will always see such accounts as ontological explorations rather than positive truths.

Theory arises in the history of consciousness. To say this is to draw attention to the fact that human consciousness has a history. Human beings, like all the higher animals, are consciously oriented toward experienced reality on which they depend for their survival. But human consciousness is unique in its relative independence of immediate circumstances. This is certainly something associated with the inadequacy of instinctive responses in man. Indeed, it seems probable that the evolution of a rational and projective consciousness in man, connected with the acquisition of language, and evidenced by the archaeological records of tools and images stretching back to the early stone age, was the prime cause of the atrophy of his instinctive responses. Possession of a rational or estimative and projective consciousness is the precondition both for the creative articulation of meaning in language and the development of social institutions. In both cases, the human faculty of symbolic expression permits the attainment of these constitutive features of social reality.

The articulation of meaning in discourse and institution building is an aspect of man's creative response to the problems of his existence. In a sense, institutions and meaning-patterns can only be separated artificially, for analytical purposes and in deference to traditional divisions between disciplines, on the basis of a distinction between verbal and non-verbal symbols. Both prove adequate responses only to the extent that they embody the results of primary reflection upon the world, though the level of conscious reflection is in many cases low. Looked at in this way, myths can be seen as first-level discursive attempts to account for the origins of thought and action patterns developed in the course of that creative involvement in reality which we call history. Mythologies, which aspire to explain reality, are part of the level Schutz called first-order constructs. They render experience meaningful rather than inquire what foundation meaning and intelligibility may have in experienced reality. Theory, on the other hand, arises in a secondary, almost inquisitorial reflection upon these first-order constructs. This is true of philosophy and the human sciences.

Philosophy originates in critical reflection upon symbols present in social reality. The fact that it takes linguistic form means that it starts with certain pre-theoretical assumptions inherent in the language structures it uses, but, building upon the capacity of language to reflect upon itself, it subjects these presuppositions to critical examination, in order to clarify what they are and how far they may be rationally justified. Theory illuminates inadequacies, verbal ambiguities, unclear connections, confusions of ontological level, present in symbolic discourse that has not been subjected to such trial. Theory reveals, through the discovery of the limits of knowledge, that the aspiration to total inclusive meaning, a vital factor in man's cognitive involvement in the world, is never achieved in anything more than an imperfect and provisional way, and then only within limits that mock the original ambition of myth.

George Steiner likens scientific progress to the opening of successive doors in Bluebeard's castle. Fearing what we may find beyond, we must yet open each door as we come to it: 'We cannot turn back. We cannot choose the dreams of unknowing. We shall, I expect, open the last door in the castle even if it leads, perhaps *because* it leads, on to realities which are beyond the reach of human comprehension and control. We shall do so with that desolate clairvoyance, so marvellously rendered in Bartok's music, because opening doors is the tragic merit of our destiny.'[16] What this could mean in the natural sciences, whether in genetic engineering or atomic physics is obvious enough, and it may be thought that Steiner's elevated, tragic tone is not appropriate to the human problems raised by sociological theory. Yet we should not forget or ignore the tension which must exist between social reality and sociological theory. Theory aspires to interpret the world and not to change it, whatever the extra-theoretical commitments of the theorist; but interpretation and analysis tend to show up the gaps between what things are and what people believe them to be. Symbolic universes are a mighty support for life, whether they are cast in mythical-religious or ideological-political form, and they will sometimes be defended to the death. Socrates was the first to pay with his life for his devotion to theory.

5 The Edge of Suspicion

Today the reputation of sociology is scandalous and not wholly unjustifiably so. Comte's grand project of a positivist science of order has foundered. The stream has split, and the rock that divides the channels is nothing less than the nature of social reality itself. Rather than scale the rock, most social scientists have been content to be carried one way or other around it. In one channel we find the enemies of theory, the hard-headed empiricists whose laboriously acquired collections of facts, justified by the rules that define respectable research, claim to prove the most trivial of hypotheses. In the other paddle the exponents of critical sociology in whom the critical dimension of theory has been swollen into a thoroughgoing rejection of the inescapable conditions of human life on earth. But the critical claim of theory is justified only when it is based in an ontological clarification of the nature of man's being in the world. Criticism must not degenerate into a cloudy universal suspicion which treats every human thought as an example of false consciousness and every institution as a deforming cast upon the body of mankind. Beyond the edge of suspicion, when its cutting work is done, we must achieve a truer conception of social reality as an embodiment of man's creative response to the pressures of existence.

Sociology is, or ought to be, a critical clarification of what is involved in building and maintaining a civilization in the face of the pressures of reality. These pressures are of various types. They include the cultural, political and military pressure that one society may bring to bear upon another, the social and social-psychological pressures inherent in the restrictive disciplines of communal existence, the pressures of natural disasters and the cognitive pressures that surface when established meaning-patterns are shaken by the unfolding of events. To these pressures man's institutional creativity responds. In this view, institutions are the objective results of the process by which man in society equips himself for action out of the resources available to him. Institutions, on the one hand, articulate a practical answer to the question of survival. On the other, their form implies statements about man and reality. The answer to any question tells us something about the nature of the question it answers and, in this, institutional 'answers' are no exception. Institutions, like language symbols, can be 'read' for what they tell us of man's being.

59

This 'reading' is, in principle, independent of the self-understanding embodied in the legitimating formulae that are part of every institution. This is the truth preserved in the positivist claim, made by Emile Durkheim among others, that people's explanations of their own behaviour are not to be given a privileged position by the sociologist. But it is a limited truth for two reasons. First, social reality is, to a considerable extent, made what it is by what people believe it to be. The sociologist cannot ignore this dimension and explain such beliefs away as 'false consciousness', for even if we could unfailingly distinguish true from false consciousness, the most outrageous of illusions has consequences which are true in the sense that they constitute part of the true nature of that which we wish to understand. The truth of a man's belief in his wife's infidelity is of no more than secondary relevance to the investigator who wants to find out why she was murdered, and this is true of such collective illusions as belief in the truth of the Protocols of the Elders of Zion. Why people believe certain things is an interesting question in itself and one that the social scientist must try to answer, but the answer he gives cannot retrospectively 'correct' the accuracy of his initial grasp of the significant surface of events. Indeed, ideologically blinkered social science gives itself away precisely because it assumes that it knows why things are so prior to any investigation of *what* they are. The Marxist who can always explain a cultural phenomenon by reference to the system of economic production is at one here with the Freudian who knows in advance of analysis that the root of an adult neurosis must lie in an infantile trauma. Secondly, no less than social science itself, self-understanding arises as a more or less adequate response to problems in the real world. The adequacy of the response, the effectiveness and even more the appropriateness of institutions in overcoming the problems of human life, is a measure of the degree to which they embody a true ontology implicit in common sense. To read the truth about man from the forms of his societies is the main task of the sort of ontologically aware social science I am advocating.

I ally my approach to sociology with that represented, for example, by Eliade in the study of religion. Eliade's approach to religious symbolism and ritual is that of a creative hermeneutics that strives to embody in discursive language the truth compactly attested in religious experience and symbol. Eliade writes:

> The historian of religions uses an empirical method of approach. He is concerned with religio-historical facts which he seeks to understand and to make intelligible to others. He is attracted to both the *meaning* of a religious phenomenon and to its *history*, he tries to do justice to both and not to sacrifice either one of them. Of course, the historian of religions also is led to systematize the results of his findings and to reflect on the structure of the religious phenomena. But then he completes his historical work as phenomenologist or philosopher of

religion. In the broad sense of the term, the science of religions embraces the phenomenology as well as the philosophy of religion. But the historian of religions *sensu stricto* can never ignore that which is historically concrete. He applies himself to deciphering in the temporally and historically concrete the destined course of experiences that arise from an irresistible human desire to transcend time and history. All authentic religious experience implies a desperate effort to disclose the foundation of things, the ultimate reality. But all expression or conceptual formulation of such religious experience is imbedded in a historical context. Consequently, these expressions and formulations become 'historical documents', comparable to all other cultural data, such as artistic creations, social and economic phenomena, and so forth. The greatest claim to merit of the history of religions is precisely its effort to decipher in a 'fact', conditioned as it is by the historical moment and cultural style of the epoch, the existential situation that made it possible.[1]

By analogy, I would maintain that in the variety of historical forms human societies take we can recognize recurrent and even permanent features. Neither man nor society is ever wholly new because, wherever his imagination may lead him, the reality to which he responds remains the same. It is tempting here to take a short cut and talk immediately of a 'natural' order of society determined by the cosmos and only rearranged in history. But this will not do. To take the short cut would be to ignore the creative dimension of human activity. The existential situation, to use Eliade's term, makes a human response possible; it does not make it happen. If I resist the temptation of talking here of a natural order it is not because I believe that there is no such thing to be discovered in social reality, but because it must not be misinterpreted to mean anything like an automatic, instinctual or mechanical response to the stimuli of the environment. Particular historical circumstances do not determine equivalent predictable human responses. At best we can say that a particular cluster of variables seems to make a certain type of response more likely. The so-called causal effect of external stimuli upon the human actor, the bread, butter and caviar of the behaviourists, is always mediated, except in the very limited range controlled by instinct, by meaning-patterns which are not themselves mere 'effects' of an environmental 'cause'. Obviously circumstances limit the range of choice open within a wider range of human possibility, both for the individual and the civilization. But, though Durkheim rightly sees such circumstances as external and constraining to the actor, they do not determine the actual choice that he will make on any occasion. This is the preserve of free and creative human subjectivity responding to an objectively existing context of society, nature and cosmos. In that response, manifested in forms of human creation that vary from poems to post offices, a genuinely novel level of reality is introduced into the world. The fact that this level of human achievement depends on something other than itself, that neither poem nor post is a creation out of nothing, argues for metaphysical modesty but not for behaviourist determinism.

History and cultural anthropology are, within the range of the science of man, the topical sciences of the novel and the unique. The subject matter of a historical or cultural anthropological study is typically constituted by one such response or linked set of responses realized as an intelligible succession of historical events or a distinctive cultural and institutional order. The historian who cannot recognize and communicate the specific differences that distinguish the First World War from all other conflicts will hardly be considered a good historian. No more would we read and respect the study of a previously unknown tribe produced by a field worker who claimed he'd seen it all before. And yet the novel and the unique is not the only field of human science. There is a bedrock of apparent permanence upon which each edifice is constructed. At this level we find not only the biological constants taken for granted in every explanation of human action, but the species of creative cultural response typified by Jonas as the tool, the image and the tomb, and the universal primary symbols identified by Eliade and by Ricoeur in their studies of religious ritual and myth.[2] These are themes for a philosophical anthropology, but, just as historical and cultural-anthropological studies point to such a general theory of man as a horizon of possibility, so philosophical anthropology finds its own horizon in ontology. Each level is more abstract than the one before but the path from the study of human actions to the mysterious outlines of a universal order is one imposed on us by the open horizons of mundane social life. Ontology is however, as Wyndham Lewis might have put it, an 'enemy' science. The very mention of it raises the hackles of both positivists and Marxist critical theorists. For positivists, ontology is an impossible discipline, an attempt to disguise the impossibility of penetrating the factual surface of reality with an imaginative but scientifically worthless metaphysical vocabulary. Consider Rudolph Carnap's lofty dismissal of metaphysics as a pretence to be something that it is not:

> The form in question is that of a system of statements which are apparently related as premises and conclusions, that is, the form of a theory. In this way the fiction of theoretical content is generated, whereas . . . there is no such content. It is not only the reader, but the metaphysician himself who suffers from the illusion that the metaphysical statements say something, describe states of affairs. The metaphysician believes that he travels in territory in which truth and falsehood are at stake. In reality, however, he has not asserted anything, but only expressed something, like an artist.[3]

Carnap's case is powerfully put and, primarily through the medium of the work of A. J. Ayer, it influenced a generation of Anglophone philosophers. But it rests upon a particular conception of what may count as a meaningful statement and without that theory of meaning it loses its potency. There are, according to Carnap, only three types of meaningful statement:

> First there are statements which are true solely by virtue of their form ('tautologies' according to Wittgenstein; they correspond approximately to Kant's 'analytic judgements'). They say nothing about reality. The formulae of logic and mathematics are of this kind. They are not themselves factual statements, but serve for the transformation of such statements. Secondly, there are negations of such statements ('contradictions'). They are self-contradictory, hence false by virtue of their form. With respect to all other statements the decision about truth and falsehood lies in the protocol sentences. They are therefore (true or false) *empirical statements* and belong to the domain of the empirical science.[4]

Carnap's position is summed up in the celebrated statement that 'the meaning of a statement lies in the method of its verification'.

Now, even given that ontological statements about the order of being are not so devoid of empirical content as Carnap suggests, it must be admitted that were his theory of meaning accepted, they would, on grounds of abstraction and generality alone, be redundant. A philosophy that defines meaning in terms of direct verifiability will have little time for such universal propositions. But there is no reason to accept such a position in the first place. Leaving aside Popper's critique of the logic of verification,[5] we may recall his point that by the criteria of a philosophy like Carnap's, which restricts meaning to verifiable or tautologous statements, the very attempt so to restrict it is meaningless because unverifiable and non-tautologous. Beyond this, though, it must be stressed that Carnap's positivist conception of philosophy and science derives from a narrow notion of the nature of these forms of discourse and, of the signifying function of language in the world.

Philosophy, outside the technical area of logic and the limited domain of the syllogism, does not consist in provable propositions but in the formulation of statements that render intelligible what was previously obscure. That some propositions are able to do this is known by experience, the same experience that teaches us that they are strictly unprovable. As an example, probably the most humanly significant one we have, consider the theological propositions concerning the divine origin of man and the world and the destiny of the soul. These are not matters susceptible to proof or refutation, and only a benighted spiritualist or atheist would think that they were, but do they not render intelligible the meaning of an existence which otherwise would make no ultimate sense, and, at least in the case of the doctrine of creation, explain an order of being which we experience but for which we could not otherwise account?

Certainly theory, in the strict sense established in the last chapter, arises as a criticism of plausible meaning-patterns embodied in myth and ideology. These forms of primary expression are subjected to what I called trial by theory. But we must understand the limits of criticism and of the sentence that the theorist may impose upon the language of myth. Plato, the greatest critic of the unjustifiable pretensions of myth to a universal wisdom, reserves a place for myth in his own philosophy. Aristotle, the most empirically-minded of the classical philosophers, admitted that as he grew older he became more preoccupied with the covert significance of the mythological tales. To justify the value of ontology we must not compare its statements with an imaginary realm of science made up of strictly verifiable statements. If verification is to survive Popper's criticism it will be in a less strict form than that admitted by Carnap. The element of doubt cannot be banished from our knowledge of the surrounding world. But where this is admitted ontology regains its place among the sciences, for its speculative discourse is guided by the same criticism of immediate experience and our attempts to express it in language.

This is significant for our conception of the human sciences whose subject matter is man's creative response to the world. Human experience of being provokes the forms of expression which the human sciences study. These forms are unlike those of lower animals in that they are not confined to automatic reactions to environmental pressures. Human expressions have a free, creative and symbolic dimension. For this reason, and because human consciousness is able to reflect upon its own processes and to communicate its conclusions through language, men express their experience in terms that possess meaning; that is to say, in terms that make transparent or intelligible previous and present experience. Human expression always involves an interpretation of what it is to exist. This is the spontaneous interpretation of an articulate being seeking to orient himself to his best advantage in a preexisting context. What, following Schutz, we have called first-order constructs, and examined in the last chapter in the form of myth, bring immediate experience to meaningful expression in symbolic forms that claim to reflect an order inherent in the object of experience. Thus first-order constructs claim to embody the truth of being, and this takes discursive form in the various accepted propositions and beliefs established in the intersubjective reality of the life-world as well as in the routine forms of socially sanctioned activity we call institutions.

However, a pattern of meaning can never do more than make sense of previous experience, and the past success of an institution which arose as a response to past events is no warrant that it will prove suitable to future requirements. Meaning, taken for granted and embodied in patterned responses, is always threatened by unfolding experience. In cognitive and institutional crises men learn that the connection between experience and expression is less secure than it might seem. The fate of Newtonian physics following the work of Einstein shows that this is as true in natural science as elsewhere. In every myth truth and fallacy are deeply intertwined. In every institution permanent human requirements are found alongside elements that seem accidental and absurd. The moment of this discovery is the birth of theory, for theory is a form of questioning that reaches back from the problematic relationship between experience and meaningful expression, through clarification of what the problem implies, to fundamental questioning of the relationship between consciousness and reality. Basic distinctions such as those between reality and illusion, the knowable and the unknowable, problem and mystery, are made explicit. Theory improves our knowledge not by extending the range of the empirically known but by sharpening our sense of the significance of that of which we are already aware. New theoretical insights bring a qualitative and not a quantitative advance, though it is possible that an advance of this type will open up a new area of empirical inquiry.

Theory, in philosophy and the sciences, is directed to the clarification of knowledge of various aspects of experienced reality. Knowledge is purged, as far as possible, of the confusions of immediate common sense. Theory develops criteria of truth by which the theorist can judge the adequacy of his discourse to the reality he attempts to interpret. At least one of these criteria, coherence, is common to every region of knowledge. Discourse that is incoherent, that embodies contradictions, cannot contribute to our knowledge of the world, since from a self-contradictory statement anything and therefore nothing can be deduced. But though we require coherence, we do not usually expect it to be complete, and the presence of incoherence in theory is a negative spur to further theoretical advance which proceeds through its elimination.

Though coherence is a requirement of theoretical discourse, it is not, outside logic and mathematics, in itself the measure of truth. As William Earle says:

> no set of judgements whatsoever as judgements divorced from apprehension or intuition can have any but an accidental relation to the truth and to reality. Again no propositional calculus, as a mere chain of sentences or verbal affirmations, can supply any guarantee whatsoever of the truth of any member of such a chain. Truth can never be posited or postulated or defined into being; it must be seen.[6]

A true proposition is coherent but it is not true because it is coherent. A proposition is only true if it adequately embodies the order of experienced reality.

This is, of course, a form of the correspondence theory of truth but a

broader one than the verificationism of the positivists. I know how difficult it is to state a correspondence theory of truth in a philosophically
water-tight way and I do not intend to attempt to do so here. I do say that a
version of the correspondence theory is logically necessary to the very
notion of true discourse. The truth of discourse rests in the adequacy of its
terms to its object, for discourse is intentional or referential speech. It is
speech about some object which is independent of the act of speaking. Discourse points to something beyond itself. For the positivist this means that
a proposition must be validated by direct reference to observable facts.
This is inadequate because there is more to reality than the observable and
the sensibly known. Consider Freud's insistence that 'fantasies possess a
psychical reality opposed to material reality', and that 'in the world of
neurosis, this psychical reality plays a dominant role'. Whatever our final
judgment of the success of Freud's enterprise we may admire the way in
which the quest for knowledge in his chosen field led him to develop a discourse adequate to the object of his attention, even if he had to transgress
against the positivist equation of the natural, the observable and the real.
It is irrelevant that he was not altogether clear that this was what he was
doing; what matters is that his need to speak of a realm of reality implied
by but not contained in the surface of events led him, in opposition to the
positivist conception of verification on the current model of the natural
sciences, to forge specific criteria for judging propositions concerning the
psyche. As Ricoeur comments in 'The Question of Proof in Freud's
Writings':

> While academic psychology does not question the difference between
> the real and the imaginary, inasmuch as its theoretical entities are all
> said to refer to observable facts and ultimately to real movements in
> space and time, psychoanalysis deals only with psychical reality and
> not with material reality. So the criterion for this reality is no longer
> that it is observable, but that it presents a coherence and a resistance
> comparable to that of material reality.[7]

This is a crucial point, for the edge of positivist suspicion cuts deepest in
the question of how we may judge the validity of statements which cannot
be corroborated by appeal to direct observation. Faced with this challenge
a philosopher and psychologist of the eminence of Karl Jaspers retreats
into the hermitage of 'the inner light' and writes that: 'While the man of
science always has universally valid criteria for his results and derives his
satisfaction from their inescapable validity, the philosopher has nothing
but the ever-subjective criterion of his own being to tell empty talk from
the talk that will awaken *Existenz*.'[8] Heidegger's appeal to the unmediated
self-revelation of Being in language is no better. The deathless moment of
truth enshrined in the supposedly non-discursive text of the poem is of
merely private significance unless in discourse we are able to clarify in

what its truth consists. And this for Heidegger is impossible, for subsequent discourse will falsify the moment of revelation.

It would be gratifying if these doubts could be answered with a measure of validity as simple as Carnap's appeal to verifiability, but this is not possible. Indeed, even the logic of scientific verification has been weighed in the balance and found wanting. The dimension of the future and our incomplete knowledge of past and present deprives the most exact technique of verification of its claim to provide indubitable knowledge. Thus the positivist attempt to set science beyond suspicion may open the way to a universal scepticism, in which Jaspers' philosophy of *Existenz* finds itself joined in its subjectivism by the very physical sciences from which it exiled itself in the first place.

At the edge of the abyss, we should recall that we are brought there only by our desire to establish a single model of objective knowledge. The claim to objective knowledge of the order of reality, without which nothing but the dryness of language distinguishes ontology from free floating fiction, is quite compatible with the recognition that there is no more a single model of knowledge than there is one level in the reality we wish to understand. Interpretative sociology, for instance, confines itself neither to the observable world of behaviour nor to the inferred level of meaning and motive. Rather, it relates both in an achieved discourse adequate to its experienced object. What this form of discourse will look like, the elements it will have to take into account, cannot be laid down a priori. Only through empirical investigation does the theorist come to learn the specific requirements of his science, overcoming the interpretative problems that the object of study puts in his way.

Against the positivist insistence on the methodological unity of science, it is necessary to restate the Aristotelian insight, developed in the methodological writings of Schutz, that the only way to acquire knowledge in any field is to develop methods and concepts suitable to its exploration. The proof of methodological adequacy is cognitive advance and not fidelity to a favoured model. If our investigation of social reality leads us into ontological concerns forbidden by the positivist then so much the worse for positivism. Furthermore, cognitive advance does not always consist either in an increase in factual knowledge or of provable propositions. Clarification of the dimensions and implications of a problem also contributes to science as a truthful account of the structure of reality and the instrument by which we orient ourselves in the world.

The recognition that truth lies in the adequation of discourse to object warrants neither the positivist criterion of verifiability nor any universal alternative. Otherwise the theorist makes the servant, method, the lord of all that man surveys. In Earle's words:

> Methodological criteria . . . are nothing but concealed ways of stipulating or defining subject matters. They can have no validity in deter-

mining what we can be aware of, what we can mean, or what can be . . . . There cannot in principle be a 'theory' of what we can cognitively mean, or of what objects we can become aware of; this can be discovered only by actually knowing what we are in fact able to mean, and there can never be any exhaustive survey or dialectical scheme which can settle that.[9]

The 'impossibility' of ontology as science turns out to be the prohibition of a line of questioning which the order of reality provokes and the order of knowledge demands.

How does this demand manifest itself in social science? The answer lies in what was said in the first chapter about the four levels of interpretation through which inquiry is drawn. The first consists in the identification of the systems of meaning by which men make sense of their lives in society. The second seeks to understand the variety of these systems in relation to historical circumstances influencing the societies in which they arise. The third relates these particular patterns to anthropologically universal symbols. And the fourth refers these humanly constituted patterns to the condition of man rooted in a reality that can neither be dreamed nor defined away. Broadly speaking, these are the levels of interpretative sociology, of history and cultural anthropology, of philosophical anthropology, and of ontology. The reality which is the object of ontology may be recognized as that which asserts itself, however thoroughly we try to banish it from consciousness.

The call for the restoration of ontology as a legitimate dimension of social scientific inquiry illustrates how far we have travelled from Comte's original programme. In that programme one factor is paramount: the desire to achieve a state of affairs in which the truths of social science will be as little a matter for dispute as those of the natural sciences. Behind the original positivist project one can identify several elements. There is admiration for the achievements of the natural sciences, a particular conception of the status of scientific fact and, not least, a political ambition to overcome the disorder and conflict of what Comte called the 'critical' era, and achieve a new age of certainty, novel in the justification of dogma by appeal to observable facts. Thus, while Comte knew that, in contrast to theological and metaphysical truth, the truth of positivist science is relative and not absolute, he believed that there would be no dispute about it because, at any given stage in the growth of knowledge, the message of the facts would ring out loud and clear. The trouble is that it does no such thing. Facts do not speak their own truth. Indeed, they can only be recognized as significant when they are placed in a framework of intelligibility.

We have travelled far from Comte's conception of a social physics but we remain close to it in our guiding anxiety. The problem of order is still central. It asserts its thematic centrality when we recognize that all sociology is, in one way or another, an investigation into why societies stay together and fall apart. However, if the problem is the same our conception of what it entails is very different. The problem of order can no longer be posed simply in terms of the adaptation of man to the world of facts and the submission of the factual world to the manipulative reasoning of man. In view of the later development of social science, there is pathos in Comte's hubristic scheme to rebuild a social order beyond criticism on the sociologists' clear insight into necessity and progress. We may, with Comte, accept the lesson of Louis de Bonald that 'There are laws governing the moral and social order as there are for the physical', and even that 'Human passions may momentarily hold back the effect of these laws, but sooner or later the invincible force of nature brings society back into conformity.' Yet this can only be true so long as nature and society continue to exist. Today this axiom can no longer be taken for granted.

On another plane, the anti-metaphysical ambition of Comte, exemplified by his wish to banish from discourse questions of ultimate cause, and the anti-theological animus that issues in the prosaic positivist cult of great predecessors and the sentimental self-worship of humanity, seems naive in an age which has recovered the pre-positivist insight that such ambitions are nothing new but exemplify modes of human thinking coeval with mankind. Political tyranny has always embodied the first and the cult of ancestors as supernatural beings the second. They are held in awe precisely because, like the artists and scientists commemorated in Comte's positivist calendar, they made the tribe what it is today by their actions and gifts.

To say on the one hand that there is an objective reality which asserts itself through the humanly created forms of language and society and, on the other, that the factual surface of this reality does not speak its own truth, is to draw attention once more to the status of sociology as an interpretative or hermeneutic discipline, one which, like textual analysis, operates at a level already occupied by products of human activity and thought. Both epistemology and hermeneutics develop as self-conscious activities in the critical questioning back from expression to experience, and from consciousness to reality. This process is stimulated by the occurrence of events in the world, sometimes the world of previous theories, which are experienced as dissonant with established meaning-patterns. Interpretative theory, therefore, is a second order discourse. It is like all discourse an attempt to express what is thinkable and sayable about experience, but strives, through the development of that self-critical character which distinguishes the use of symbols in science and philosophy, to express the truth of reality in a way that previous attempts have failed to do. The problem is that there is no single criterion of correct interpretation. The field of the human sciences is, in Ricoeur's phrase, that of the 'conflict of interpretations'.[10]

Consider, in the light of my remarks on ontology, the following passage from Theodore Adorno's *Negative Dialectics:*

> If ontology were possible at all, it would be possible in an ironic sense, as the epitome of negativity. What remains equal to itself, the pure identity, is the worst. The mythical doom is timeless. Philosophy has been its secularization, in thrall to the doom in so far as its gigantic euphemisms would reinterpret the immutable as the good, down to the theodicies of Leibniz and Hegel. If one were drafting an ontology in accordance with the basic state of facts, of the facts whose repetition makes their state invariant, such an ontology would be pure horror. An ontology of culture, above all, would have to include where culture as such went wrong; a philosophically legitimate ontology would have more of a place in construing the culture industry than in construing Being. Good would be nothing but what has escaped from ontology.[11]

Adorno is the marvellously percipient product of a tradition of Marxist and Hegelian criticism. This tradition, which issues largely from Feuerbach's reversal of the claim of Genesis that man is made in the image of of God, represents, in the field of social science, the main current of that hermeneutics of suspicion identified by Ricoeur in his book on Freud.

I shall examine the Marxist critical tradition in the next chapter, concentrating particularly on the philosophers of the Frankfurt school, Adorno himself, Max Horkheimer and Herbert Marcuse, in whom the sense of critical relationship to ontology is especially developed. For the moment, to set the scene for that encounter I shall summarize the distinction between restorative and suspicious or demystifying hermeneutics which, according to Ricoeur, bisects the field of interpretations.

A restorative hermeneutics, as represented for instance by the phenomenology of religion practised by Eliade; Van der Leeuw. Leenhardt and Ricoeur himself in *The Symbolism of Evil*, conceive the task of interpretation as the recovery or recollection of the meaning of religious symbols. The assumption behind this approach is that a truth is embodied in the obscurity of the symbol, and may be uncovered and communicated by interpretation. In the phenomenology of religion we employ what Husserl called the *epoché*. That is, we suspend belief and disbelief in the literal meaning of terms in order to recover a second intended meaning. Reflective philosophy treats religious symbolism as a first-order hermeneutic in which man embodies a truth about his relationship to transcendent reality. 'Reflection', Ricoeur writes, 'is the appropriation of our effort to exist and of our desire to be, through the works which bear witness to that effort and desire.'[12] A restorative hermeneutics, therefore, is a stage in the quest for an adequate ontology of human existence. In contrast to Heidegger in *Being and Time*, Ricoeur believes that such an ontology must be approached through analysis of achieved primary

symbolic systems rather than through direct analysis of the essential structures of man's everyday being; 'reflection must become interpretation
because I cannot grasp the act of existing except in signs scattered in the
world. That is why a reflective philosophy must include the results,
methods, and presuppositions of all the sciences that try to decipher and
interpret the signs of man.'[13]

But restoration or recollection of meaning is only one possible axis of
interpretation. If a symbol may be interpreted in order to disclose an
implicit ontological truth, it may also be interpreted as an exercise in
unconscious self-deceit. Consciousness may, as in the works of Freud,
Marx and Nietzsche, be treated as false consciousness. The symbols constituted by consciousness then become veils of illusion cast over a savage
truth that man will not face. I will not follow Ricoeur further on this point
except to note that he does not regard the conflict between restorative and
suspicious hermeneutics as without possible resolution. The restoration
of meaning, *anamnesis* as a recollection of an experience of being, and the
confrontation with bare reality demanded by those masters of suspicion
and demystification for whom the sought order of being is but a crutch for
man and an excuse for the horrors of the world, interact creatively.
Through interaction, the confrontation between restoration and
reduction, Ricoeur sees the possibility of a purified vision of truth.
Though the edge of suspicion cuts into the naive trust in the truth of
consciousness and the order of the cosmos, there may still be an ontological truth beyond the edge of suspicion.

But at once Adorno's challenge recurs: 'The ontological need can no
more guarantee its object than the agony of the starving assures them of
food.'[14] This is so, but it might be better to talk of an ontological imposition than an ontological need with its ambiguous sense of subjective
desire and objective necessity. I will want to argue towards the objective
pole, toward the recognition of ontology as a part of the order of knowledge and a source of insights into the order of life. But first we must
inspect the ground on which the masters of sociological suspicion stand.

6 The Call from Beyond

Karl Marx is the master of suspicion in modern social science. His critique of consciousness and the realm of values is less radical than Nietzsche's. His dissection of culturally embodied truths is less shocking than Freud's. They are all the more socially effective for that. Marx, unlike the other two, demonstrates to dissatisfied men that the subjectively desirable is objectively necessary. The uncomfortable Nietzschian doctrines of eternal recurrence and the will to power have no strict equivalents in Marxian thought. No more has the Freudian equation between repression and civilization. For Marxism, like the Hegelian idealism to which it owes so much, is a philosophy of irreversible process, and in the Marxist theory of history the irreversibility of human action in time is conceived as a path that leads us beyond the ontological level of which Freud and Nietzsche speak. In Marxism ontology is swallowed up in history, and epistemology in a critical sociology of knowledge. The 'stages of history', each characterized by the prevalence of a particular mode of production, are the Marxist equivalents of the rungs of the ladder which the shamans of Siberia climb in search of the divine vision. But while the shaman returns to earth, the irreversibility of time and the impermanence of every established earthly order mean that for man in history there is no such return. For most Marxists this is an optimistic doctrine, and much of the ideological appeal of Marx rests in the optimism, but, as the work of Adorno and Horkheimer shows, a pessimism bordering on despair is no less possible. Adorno and Horkheimer provide, as it were, an immanent critique of Marxist optimism. To Marx's claim that: 'The philosophers have only interpreted the world, in various ways; the point is to change it', Adorno replies, in the opening sentence of *Negative Dialectics;* 'Philosophy, which once seemed obsolete, lives on because the moment to realize it was missed.'[1] The significance of this dialogue becomes clear when we examine the central stem of Marxist thinking.

In *Ludwig Feuerbach and the End of Classical German Philosophy,* Engels set out to show how his and Marx's theory grew out of the German idealist tradition. The book ends with the famous statement: 'The German working-class movement is the inheritor of German classical philosophy.' Much of the book examines the significance and limitations

72

of Feuerbach's materialist metamorphosis of Hegelian idealism. The generation of Marxist theorists which succeeded Engels stressed the significance of materialism in the genesis of Marxism and played down the properly Hegelian inheritance. Engels, by contrast, made no such mistake.

In *Ludwig Feuerbach* he not only paid tribute to the genius of Hegel but identified the characteristic of Hegelian philosophy which is of abiding significance to anyone seeking to understand the underlying spirit of Marxism. The 'great fundamental truth' which he and Marx 'freed from the idealist trimmings which with Hegel had prevented its consistent execution', is this:

> The great basic thought that the world is not to be comprehended as a complex of ready-made *things*, but as a complex of processes, in which things apparently stable no less than their mind images in our heads, the concepts, go through an uninterrupted change of coming into being and passing away, in which, in spite of all seeming accidentality and of all temporary retrogression, a progressive development asserts itself in the end.

Engels contrasted the Hegelian approach to reality with 'The old method of investigation which Hegel calls "metaphysical", which preferred to investigate *things* as given, as fixed and stable.' This method Engels claimed had been superseded by scientific advances which permitted us to pass beyond the analysis of the given thing to the 'systematic investigation of the changes which these things undergo in nature itself'.[2] Science had ceased to be the investigation of fixed properties in interaction and had become the discovery of a total process in which all such properties were destined to pass away into higher forms.

Nietzsche once said that German thought prefers Becoming to Being. By this criterion Engels is a very German thinker. But what is true of Engels is also true of the whole Marxist school where it remains faithful to the basic conception of reality as a historical process in which nothing is finally fixed or stable, a process in which man's nature changes reflexively to the changes that come about in the world about him, and in which these changes eventually come under his own control as a result of his growing mastery of nature. Thus, the Marxist thinker who refuses to accept Adorno's suspicious rejection of all ontology will have a very different ontology from the traditional attempt to explore the substantially suprahistorical order of being.

This point is illuminated in Georg Lukács' ambitious final work *Toward the Ontology of Social Being*. Lukács' aim there was to provide Marxist philosophy with the explicit theory of being it had hitherto lacked. There are two major elements. One is a restatement of Marx's views on the priority of being over consciousness; the other is an insistence on the essential historicity of being. Lukács writes:

> Substance, as the ontological principle of persistence through change, has certainly lost its old sense as an exclusive opposite to becoming, but it now acquires a new and more profound validity, in so far as persistence comes to be conceived as that which continually maintains itself, renews itself and develops in the real complexes of reality, in so far as continuity as an internal form of motion of the complex makes the abstract and static persistence into a concrete persistence within becoming. This is true even for complexes of an inorganic kind, and forms the principle of reproduction in the organism and society. This transformation of the former static concept of substance into a dynamic one, of one that downgrades the world of appearance for the sake of the exclusive and single substance into the substantiality of dynamic complexes that differ so greatly among themselves, is indicated by all the new achievements of science, while these refute any kind of simple relativism, subjectivism, etc. This however has the further consequence . . . that the concept of substance ceases to stand in an exclusive antithesis to historicity, as it does most significantly with Spinoza. On the contrary, continuity in persistence, as the existential principle of dynamic complexes, demonstrates ontological tendencies towards historicity as a principle of being itself.[3]

In fact, this historicity of being turns out to be not merely *a principle* but *the exclusive principle* of any possible Marxist ontology, and as a result Marxists fail to take into account any element of reality that cannot adequately be treated as a historical process. No one who fails to see the extent to which this view is a direct development of Hegel's idealist historicism will ever understand the nature of Marxist thought. For the truth at the heart of Marxism is that, in spite of its claims to be called materialist, it is in fact a variety of the German idealism it claimed to transcend.

It is worth dwelling on the interaction of materialist and idealist elements in Marxian thought in general before passing on to examine the metaphysical assumptions that underlie the thought of Marcuse. Marx himself was anxious to distinguish his materialism from anything that went by that name in the past. Though he paid tribute to materialist predecessors from Democritus to Helvetius and Feuerbach, he stressed that his own theory fundamentally differed from theirs precisely to the extent that it was a historical rather than a metaphysical or ontological materialism. Marx did not reject metaphysical materialism, the view that matter is the ultimate substance of the universe and that what we call mind or spirit is epiphenomenal and ultimately explicable in terms of the interaction between material particles; in fact he showed considerable sympathy with it. But, as he wrote in the first of the *Theses on Feuerbach:*

The chief defect of all hitherto existing materialism ... is that the thing, reality, sensuousness, is conceived only in the form of the *object* or of *contemplation*, but not as *sensuous human activity, practice*, not subjectively. Hence in contradistinction to materialism, the *active* side was developed abstractly by idealism — which, of course, does not know real sensuous activity as such.[4]

Historical, as opposed to metaphysical, materialism is less a theory of the basic constitution of the universe than a belief that the movement of human history and the character of human societies at any given stage of that history is determined by the external material environment.

This view, far from being incompatible with a certain form of idealism, can be seen as the only appropriate completion of it. Historical materialism is a theory which places before man a realistic chance of fulfilling the fundamental project of Hegelian idealism, to bring being into harmony with thinking. Since Marx was clear that: 'It is not the consciousness of men that determines their being, but, on the contrary, their social being that determines their consciousness',[5] this statement needs some justification, which can readily be provided if we relate Marx's view to that of his idealistic predecessors, and Hegel in particular.

Hegel's idealism, in contrast to that of Kant, is a historical idealism, Kant taught that the intelligible character of the phenomenal world is inexplicable unless we accept that its intelligible structures are imposed by the mind itself, Hegel believed that the process of reality is one in which the Universal Spirit or Mind *(Geist)* progressively becomes conscious of the object-world as its own product. Behind the known and knowable world of phenomena Kant taught that there was an unknowable world of things in themselves, and the arguments for its unknowability preclude the possibility of metaphysics as, in Aristotle's phrase, the science of being as being. Behind this same phenomenal world Hegel argued that there is only the creative power of the Universal Subject, whose progress to self-consciousness is the process of reality itself. The process finds completion in the moment of self-consciousness when the subject becomes aware of the true status of the object as the product of his own activity.

In Hegelian terms, the reconciliation of subject and object, in the realization that the object is a manifestation of subject, is achieved at the moment the subject becomes conscious of it — that is, in Hegel's philosophy. It was Marx's specific contribution to show the incompleteness of this view. So long as the realization that the object-world is the product of subjective activity is limited to the theoretical realm of contemplation, to philosophy in its traditional sense, the material world on which man, the worldly subject, acts and which acts on him remains alien to him. This material world is man's real object and it cannot be regarded as reconciled with his subjectivity until it is brought under his rational control, to be moulded to his needs.

It is essential here to disentangle the materialist and idealist strands in Marx's argument. The materialist strand is clear in Marx's view that the possibility of bringing the object-world under human control is determined by the state of man's relationship to nature. The state of his being in relation to the natural world determines the very possibility of achieving rational control. But this relationship is not unchanging. Necessity, in the form of material scarcity, forces man to act upon the world, and through such action the relationship is changed. Nature is transformed by human activity and, to the extent that the problems of immediate scarcity are overcome, the being on which man and human consciousness are said to depend itself becomes a being structured or produced by human activity. This is the significance of the shift from 'being' to 'social being' in Marx's statement that it is 'social being that determines . . . consciousness'. Thus, an apparently materialist premise, that man depends on and is conditioned by a natural, material world, leads to the idealist conclusion that being may be moulded to the demands of human reason.

This depends upon human progress in achieving dominance over the natural environment; but is a result of the human need to overcome the scarcity of necessary goods. In achieving it, men evolve relations of production, forms of social organization, suited to the stage reached in the evolution of their productive powers. The contrast between evolution at the level of the forces of production — an evolution which may like the evolution of the natural world proceed by mutation — and revolution at the level of the relations of production, arises in the fact that, once created, political and cultural institutions take a fixed form. This form is shattered periodically by the developing productive forces. Men may imagine the form of institutions to be natural, God-given or immutable, but in fact, Marx claims, it is man-made and historically transient. One of the major insights which he claimed for his theory is the revelation of the man-made character of institutions — even of social phenomena as apparently autonomous as the laws of the market. Marxism reveals to man the worker the absolute dependence of the nature of the object-world on his potentially, rationally controllable activity; just as Hegelianism had revealed the object of thought as the product of mind. Both attempt, at different levels, to realize the imperial ambition of idealism: to reduce the object to a manifestation of subjectivity.

Bearing this in mind, let us examine the quotation from the *Preface to a Contribution to the Critique of Political Economy* cited above: 'It is not the consciousness of men that determines their being, but, on the contrary, their social being that determines their consciousness.' The thesis that man's social being determines his consciousness is unequivocally materialist only in so far as man's social being is not the result of human rational activity. One does not cease to be an idealist in maintaining it if, like Marx, he sees the nature of social being as the product of activity which can, in principle, be directed in accord with the dictates of subjective reason. As the forces of production develop, the possibilities of such accord are steadily increased. The chains of non-human nature are loosened through the reduction of the non-human to a form imposed by men. The underlying spirit of Marx's work is idealist because, in Marxism, the form of reality is ultimately the product of subjectivity, of men themselves. Historical materialism is a variety of idealism since in its theory, history is seen as the process of disintegration of apparently stable natures or forms in being. However the world originated, it is recreated to its essence in the image of man the maker. The joker in Marx's materialist pack turns out to be the *Geist* in the machine, and the joker always wins the play. Let us consider further the term 'essence'. As a term, essence in traditional philosophy designates that which makes something itself and not something else. Thus essences, which permit us to identify things for what they are, also constitute a realm of limiting realities, for we cannot make a thing cease to be itself without making it cease to be. The transmutation of natures was formerly seen as the concern of the magician rather than the philosopher, who, like the rest of us, was compelled to take account of things as they essentially are. Thomas Molnar illustrates the contrast in his discussion of the decisive difference between Plato and Hegel:

> 'for the first, philosophical speculation, the process of thinking, can never be aimed at the transformation of what is thought about, that is, of reality, of the constitution of being; only the soul, that is, man, can change . . . , develop a different view of reality, by deepening his understanding of it, by turning from error to truth. For Hegel, on the other hand, reality itself changes, it gradually becomes what the philosopher, as the privileged representative of the *Geist*, wants it to become, or better, what he understands as being in the nature of reality to become. Plato's human conversion is a *metanoia*, a change of mind and attitude with regard to existence prompted by contact with it and reflection on it; Hegel's change is a *metastasis* that assumes that starting from subjective criteria and will . . . , reality itself undergoes the foreseen and willed transformations.[6]

Hegel recognized that there is a realm rightly and exclusively designated 'reality', and, at the same time, believed that the truth contained in his philosophy was the unique truth of that reality. Nothing can be more important to the understanding of the significance of his work and of that of Marx, than to know what he thought to be the essence of the real. Engels was right in identifying this essence in Hegelianism as a 'complex of processes', 'an uninterrupted change of coming into being and passing away'. 'The truth', as Hegel says in *The Phenomenology of Mind*, 'is the whole. The whole, however, is merely the essential nature reaching its completeness through the process of its own development. Of the Absolute it must be said that it is essentially a result, that only at the end is it what it is in its very truth; and just in that consists its nature, which is to be actual, subject, or self-becoming, self-development.'[7]

A century or so later Lukács took up the idea that 'the truth is the whole' in order to rescue Marxist thought from the toils of a narrowly interpreted economic determinism. Only a few years later Adorno stated, from the standpoint of the same tradition, that: 'The whole is untrue'. Yet, in a manner appropriate to a school that prides itself on its mastery of dialectics, these positions must not be conceived as irreconcilable opposites. In Marxism, as in Hegelian philosophy, the true is the whole when our conception of the whole embodies the totality of the process by which that which is actually so at any particular moment has come into being and will pass away. In contrast, the whole is untrue when what we envisage is merely the actually existing state of affairs. The untrue whole is the world established about us; the true is the historical totality which bears and condemns all such kingdoms to perish until the final attainment of reason and freedom.

This idealist philosophy of process denies final reality to fixed determinations of things as they may be identified here and now. It appeals to a young radical aiming not so much to comprehend the world as to change it, for it makes of the processes of change the only proper object of rational comprehension. This transformation of the order of being into an order of historical process is a more significant influence on Marx's thought than the static metaphysical materialism which teaches that we are merely complex effects of inhuman and immutable causes. Marx could with Hegel reject the doctrine of essences as limiting realities, while shifting the *locus* of the process from the speculative realm of the World Spirit to the level of practical human activity. In this way human labour and political action could be treated as the fundamental creative principles of the world as it is to be. No one wrote before Marx: 'The philosophers have only interpreted the world in various ways; the point, however, is to change it.' Apart from the Marxo-Hegelian perspective outlined above, the sentence is not one of great significance. An Aristotelian would point out that the tasks of interpreting and changing cannot be contrasted in this way; interpretation is necessary in order that we should know the ways in which the world may or may not be changed. With this point the Marxist might concur, but no further. For if he asked the Aristotelian what it was that delimited the possibilities of changing the world, the reply would be in terms of the nature of things, the essential character of those beings, human and non-human, animal, vegetable and mineral, with which our existence puts us in relation. The contrast between interpreting and changing the world only acquires the significance suggested by Marx's words when it is recognized that correct interpretation depends ultimately upon identification of ontological natures or essences, while change, as conceived by Marx, depends on the dissolution of all such constancies in the creative corrosion of history, a process now itself within the potential control of human reason. If this argument seems too abstract, consider the reaction of a Marxist politician to an objection to his plans based on the common-sense observation that 'human nature just isn't like that'. He will reply, in accord with the sixth of the *Theses on Feuerbach*, that 'there is no such thing as a determinate human nature apart from the ensemble of social relations that form it, and, therefore, what you say, however true of man today, will not be true in the future.'

In theory, of course, the Marxist will claim that he allows there are limitations to human nature (if he does not, it is hard to see why people should not be equally satisfied in any social system, and this would undermine the motive for political action), but it is difficult to see how he is ever to identify what these might be and, therefore, the limits of possible transformation in human nature and society. I do not wish to imply that our knowledge of human nature is ever actually complete. Reality is, as Voegelin puts it, a mystery in the process of unfolding and thus the limits of our actual knowledge of potentiality are quite untranscendable. But this is not to say that we are clueless, for history, which never finally tells us what man is, does at least reveal the boundaries at which he arrives in his creative effort to achieve a meaningful existence. It tells us also that some of these frontiers of achievement, such as the incompleteness of knowledge itself, are constitutive of human existence at every possible moment of history. They must therefore be regarded as supra-historical ontological factors in our experience of reality. The Hegelian and Marxist reduction of ontology to history obscures this and, with it, the prudential wisdom of the classical doctrine of essence. Consequently the Marxist cannot distinguish between real possibility and fantasy, a distinction founded in the recognition of being as a field in which timeless truth manifests itself in transient appearance.

Once again the roots of this lie in Hegelian idealism, as Marcuse's discussion of Hegel's *Logik* in *Reason and Revolution* makes clear.[8] At an early stage in his intellectual development Hegel distinguished between 'understanding', which 'conceives a world of finite entities, governed by the principle of identity and opposition', the realm of fixed natures, and reason or speculative thinking, which conceives 'the intellectual and moral world not as a totality of fixed and stable relations, but "as a becoming, and its being as a product and a producing".'[9] Thus the essence of each thing is regarded as the fulfilling of the process which it undergoes. To know what a thing is in itself is to comprehend it as a process that negates what it appears to be here and now: 'Every particular existent is essentially different from what it could be if its potentialities were realized.' The potentialities are not given in the appearance of the thing but in the 'notion' which the reason develops in order to comprehend that process. The truth is a speculative truth which always 'negates' the finitude of things as they appear to be.[10] The implication of truth in appearance, which is a presupposition of all hermeneutics, is radically transformed here to signify that the true nature of anything that actually exists is the speculative negation of what it seems to be. If the gulf between essence and appearance is characteristic of Platonism, the view that the two are in absolute contradiction is a specifically Hegelian position which Marx and his followers made the dialectical excuse for identifying Utopia with reality.

In this scheme, essence ceases to be the *locus* of the inherent limitations of each being. It is identified with that which reaches beyond these boundaries. This has to be remembered whenever a Marxo-Hegelian talks of 'potentiality' or 'real possibility'. How can one understand what real possibility, as opposed to imagined fantasy, might be unless he has an awareness of the untranscendable limitations of every finite being? This is the metaphysic implicit in Marx's project to change the world, to move from the realm of necessity to the realm of freedom. Freedom only moves beyond necessity, rather than operating in the limited but real space within it, when the guarantors of necessity, the nature of things and their relationship in being, are transformed, and they can only be transformed if their essence is to change from what they appear to be, if being is ultimately a process of indeterminates.

But things do have identifiable natures which remain constant in change. Philosophy can be construed as an attempt to make sense of the experience of reality as a process of that which is not only process. This point is well expressed in Voegelin's discussion of Parmenides in *Anamnesis*. He writes:

> Being is experienced not only as a stream but also reveals abiding and recurrent forms that abide in the midst of flux, the nature of being as becoming must necessarily be supplemented by its characterization as abiding and recurrent form. Experiences of this kind motivate the speculation about being as eternally immutable. When they are reinforced by the experience of transcendence, they can elevate the character of permanence of being to the point of truth of being before which 'coming-into-being is quenched' (Parmenides B8, 21). This truth, if not logically compelling but still a compelling vision, indeed results in an inclination of philosophy toward form as the true being. Since the original insight into the nature of being as a coming-to-be goes back to the primary experience of the cosmos and its expression in the myth, one can define metaphysics, inasmuch as it narrows the insight to the form-matter pattern, as the extreme anti-mythical form of philosophizing.[11]

As philosophy endeavours to restate the problem of the *arché*, or origin of being, in a critical discourse freed of the narrative of cosmogonic myth, terms like form and essence express that which abides in the process of experienced reality. The classical doctrine of essence is developed specifically to explain the experience of abiding and recurrent forms. It is interesting to see how Marcuse, a philosophically aware disciple of Hegel and Marx, deals with that doctrine and its development through the ages.

'The Concept of Essence', first published in 1936, is one of those early essays of Marcuse which, as Alasdair MacIntyre has said, are on certain points 'more explicit than anything in the later work'.[12] Marcuse begins by stating that 'there are fundamental concepts whose metaphysical character sets them far apart from the sociohistorical roots of thought.' One of these is essence. But such concepts are not to be understood in their own terms: 'Their metaphysical character betrays more than it conceals. For so much of men's real struggles and desires went into the metaphysical quest for an ultimate unity, truth and universality of Being that they could not have failed to find expression in the derived forms of the philosophical tradition.'[13] There is no question here of accepting metaphysics as anything but a disguise for something else.

For a moment Marcuse speaks the language of his former master, Martin Heidegger. Talking of Plato's theory of ideas, he notes that: 'it was an outcome of the quest for the unity and universality of Being in view of the multiplicity and changeability of beings.' But

> This problem was not one of epistemology alone. For when the unity in multiplicity, the universal, is conceived as what truly exists, critical and ethical elements enter into the concept of essence. The isolation of the one universal Being is connected to that of authentic Being from inauthentic, of what should be and can be from what is. The Being of things is not exhausted in what they immediately are; they do not appear as they could be. The form of their immediate existence is imperfect when measured against their potentialities, which comprehension reveals as the image of their essence. Their *eidos*, or Idea, becomes the criterion by means of which the distance between existence and what it could be, its essence, is measured in each case.[14]

The language of 'authenticity' is Heideggerian but the gloss Marcuse imposes on Plato (and later on Aristotle) is more typically Hegelian. Plato, in Marcuse's reading, is a proto-Hegel for whom the realm of essence is less the level of pure intelligibility in which imperfect material beings participate by resemblance to immaterial exemplars, than the picture of what these beings could become. Because the essence of things is what they might become, Marcuse believes that 'the ancient theory of essence was impelled by the unrest of the unresolved tension between essence and existence.' A sounder view is that the development of the theory of essence by Plato, Aristotle and their followers was motivated primarily by the need to render philosophy a more adequate tool for tracing the intelligibility of the world. In this view the Christian philosophy of the Middle Ages, which Marcuse accuses of pacifying 'the critical consciousness of this antithesis (between essence and existence) in an onto-theological principle,' is the legitimate successor of the classical schools. If Thomas Aquinas regarded the distinction between essence and existence as 'a structural law of the created world', it is no less true that Aristotle viewed it as a feature of the eternally existing universe of his philosophy. What Marcuse writes of the tension between essence and existence is true, not of Plato and Aristotle, but of the later Gnostics who drew upon Platonic ideas to formulate a theology of union with a spiritual essence as a means of deliverance from the imperfect world of existence.

In his discussion of the doctrine of essence from Descartes to Husserl, Marcuse strives to relate its development to the history of the bourgeois world. Descartes' philosophy, which takes the *ego cogito* as, an 'indubitably existing particle of the world' and at the same time . . . 'the only springboard into the world', is symptomatic of the historically progressive tendencies of the bourgeoisie.

> Only when the ego as something really existing in the world becomes the first certainty in the realm of beings can its reason provide the critical standard of real knowledge and serve as the organon for the ordering of life. And only so long as reason is constitutively directed toward empirically given 'material' can its spontaneity be more than mere imagination. Once this connection between rational thought and spatio-temporal reality is severed, the 'interest of freedom' disappears completely from philosophy.[15]

For Marcuse, the philosophy of Husserl represents this latter development, for in Husserl's phenomenology the realm of essence is open to investigation only in the reduced sphere of transcendental consciousness, where 'The essential truths that make their appearance in this dimension "do not contain the slightest assertion about facts, and thus from them alone not even the most meagre factual truth can be derived".'[16]

The line from Descartes to Husserl passes through Kant. Kant taught that 'The intelligible essence of everything, and especially of man, stands . . . outside of every causal connection, as it stands outside of or above time. Thus it can never be determined by anything that has gone before it, in that it rather is prior, not so much temporally as logically, to everything else that is or becomes within it.'[17] But for Kant the free essence of man, which resides in his reason, is limited to 'furnishing the determining grounds of actions, to "beginning" them. Once begun, actions enter the unbreakable causal nexus of natural necessity.' The idealist tradition, leading to Husserl, stabilizes the uncritical element in this theory of essence, as, in a different way, the anti-essentialist teachings of positivism did. 'When all facts are indiscriminately held to be essential, and when each fact is indiscriminately held to be an essence, philosophy's attitude is fundamentally identical.'[18] But there had been another way forward from Kant, which involved the formulation of a dynamic theory of essence. This was the path taken by Hegel and pursued outside the realm of philosophy by Marx.

Marxist materialist theory is said to take up

> the concept of essence where philosophy last treated it as a dialectical concept in Hegel's *Logic*. The critical impulses in the theory of essence, abandoned by (Husserlian) eidetics as well as positivism, have been incorporated into materialist theory. Here, however, the concept of essence takes on a new form. This theory conceived concern with the essence of man as the task of a rational organization of society, to be achieved through practice that alters its present form. Materialist theory thus transcends the given state of fact and moves toward a different potentiality, proceeding from immediate appearance to the essence that appears in it. But here appearance and essence become members of a real antithesis arising from the particular historical structure of the social process of life. The essence of man and of things appears within that structure; what men and things could genuinely be appears in 'bad', 'perverted' form. At the same time, however, appears the possibility of negating this perversion and realizing in history that which could be.[19]

Voegelin subtitled his essay on Hegel 'A Study in Sorcery'. In the passage just cited Marcuse is playing the sorcerer's apprentice with a vengeance. If in Hegelian logic opposites melt into one another and the truth of everything contradicts its appearance, then Marcuse's account of how the concept of essence becomes the legitimate inheritance of the Marxist revolutionary movement is exemplary of its type. The concept of essence, as taken up by Marxism, means precisely the opposite of what it did in classical philosophy. The 'critical and ethical' elements, which Marcuse finds in the concept of essence from the beginning, have driven out the representation of constancy in being which the doctrine of essence is supposed to explain. Plato's clear ontological differentiation between levels of being is transmuted by the alchemy of Marcuse into the logic of historical progress. Even Aristotle's teachings on act and potential are fundamentally transformed, when potentiality is conceived as a property of the historical totality rather than as something ever present in each actual member of the species. Marcuse's metaphysics turn out to be anti-metaphysics, in that a science of being-as-being is left without any object apart from a speculatively conceived totality of history. What remains is a more or less blind process which man will one day be able to direct as he wills.

Many Marxists would argue that, while there is some truth in this reading of Marcuse's thought, it is inapplicable to that of Marx. Alfred Schmidt, for instance, emphasizes that Marx opposed Hegel's teachings on the ultimate identity of subject and object. Such a philosophy in practical terms means the total subjugation of object to subject or, in Marxist materialist terms, the reduction of nature to the forms imposed by human activity and, thereby, the transcendence of natural, objective limitations by man's activity and nature. 'Whenever Marx writes of the "slumbering potentialities" of nature, he is always referring to the objective possibility, inherent in nature, of its transfer into definite human use-values.'[20]

To see the significance of this apparent limitation, we must remember that the form of the Marxist doctrine of labour is closely modelled on the Hegelian doctrine of the world-creating universal Subject, of which it is, in a sense, merely the earthy, practical application. The Hegelian epistemology of creative subject survives in Marxism in a changed form, though labour rather than thought is the level on which creation and transformation occur. On epistemological issues concerning the relationship between subject and object, Schmidt argues that Marx upheld, 'an intermediate position between Kant and Hegel, which can only be fixed with difficulty.' For while his critique of Hegel's philosophy of identity between Subject and Object led him back toward Kant and the noumenal world of 'things in themselves', his acceptance of post-Kantian historicism led him to conceive this non-identity as a changing relationship in which the historical subject, man working on matter, steadily asserts itself 'in increasing measure over the material provided by nature'.[21]

Human labour plays in this theory the same formative or creative role as conceptualization does in post-Kantian idealism. The epistemological obsession of idealism acquires a materialist, ontological, disguise; it becomes a theory of the changing form and capacity of man's powers of production. This is borne out in Schmidt's own judgement that 'The question of the possibility of knowing the world only had meaning for Marx on the assumption that the world was a human "creation". We only really know what a natural thing is when we are familiar with all the industrial and experimental-scientific arrangements which permit its creation.'[22]

Marx's exact epistemological position is, as Schmidt says, only 'fixed with difficulty'. This is scarcely surprising. Marx was not interested in the sort of philosophical exegesis that could make his position clear. But, in turn, the reason for this is not difficult to see and, once seen, it reveals the nature of his philosophical assumptions clearly. Marx does not deal directly with epistemology because, in his theory, the ways of knowing, and what is known, essentially alter with the process of man's historical development. Thus epistemology is transformed into a historicist sociology of knowledge in which what is known and how are explained away as functions of the evolution of production. Behind this *ersatz* theory of knowledge, as behind every epistemology, lie the metaphysical assumptions of the theorist. Even when, like Marx, the theorist fails to make these assumptions explicit, they can be discovered by asking of the theory (whether epistemological, sociological, psychological or historical), what must be true of reality for this theory to give us a true representation of the position? What is the ontological composition of a world where this is true?

Once the question is posed, the character of Marx's theory is plain. For Marx epistemology is as uninteresting as the metaphysics of finite beings dismissed by Hegel, because the reality of the nature on which man acts and the nature of the actor himself are conceived as open processes whose essence is to change. That is why, though the Marxist tradition pays lip service to the significance of natural limitations, it always dismisses ontological arguments drawn from the actual, observable, present nature of man and things. In the generation or so after Marx's death in 1883 the omnipotence of history and the potential empire of rational man were conceived in terms of a rigid historical determinism, and Marx himself gave his successors ample reason for doing so. A Russian critic of the first edition of *Das Kapital* wrote that 'Marx only troubles himself about one thing: to show by rigid scientific investigation the necessity of successive determinate orders of social conditions . . . Marx treated the social movement as a process of natural history, governed by laws not only independent of human will, consciousness and intelligence but on the contrary determining that will, consciousness and intelligence.' Marx so liked this interpretation that he quoted it approvingly in the *Preface* to the second edition of the book, and not surprisingly this interpretation predominated in the years after the master's death.

Each special science, it is commonly said, grows out of a central philosophical stem from which, as it develops, it steadily detaches itself. For the Marxist theorists of the *Second International*, Kautsky, Plekhanov, and the Austro-Marxists, Marxism was just such a science. They developed Marx's 'materialist' appropriation of the Hegelian philosophy of flux and process as a science of immutable laws governing the history of human societies in the same way that natural selection governed the evolution of species. These laws operated at the level of the economy. Here, the progressive increase in man's productive powers came periodically into conflict with the political, social and intellectual institutions developed by society at an earlier stage. In other words, the social superstructure (political institutions, philosophies etc.) rested on the substructure of the economy and a change in the latter would cause a long term change in the former. They studied history assiduously to discover instances in which movements in the superstructure could be traced back to changes in the mode and relations of production. A classical example is provided by Kautsky's statement: 'The Reformation is nothing more than the ideological expression of far-reaching changes on the contemporary European wool-market.'[23] Thus the superstructure, in which every social or intellectual institution but the purely economic was included, was rigidly determined by the development of the economy.

This, however, was only half the determinist story. There was also the determination of the course of history by the dynamism of the same productive forces. The long-term growth in man's power to exploit nature and make it serve his needs, in which the progressive direction of history was contained in bud, had already broken the institutional bonds of feudal society and released the pressures that found expression in the capitalist mode of production and the bourgeois state. Now it was the turn of capitalism to be exploded by the pressures which it had itself generated. A system based upon the private ownership of property was an anachronism, blocking the full utilization of the economic power it contained. Furthermore, the capitalist system produced for its own benefit a growing class which had no interest in its survival and everything to gain from its fall: the proletariat. Eventually the build-up of these pressures would result in a more or less violent revolution out of which would emerge socialism. Socialism was conceived as an industrial system in which the relations of production, the political and economic institutions of society, had been brought into line with the progress already made at the level of economic production.

The theory was neat but, as time went on, it required revision. First, the proletariat did not seem to be getting more destitute as Marx had expected. This was explained by interpreting Marx's words to mean nothing more than an impoverishment relative to an increasingly wealthy bourgeoisie. More serious, Marx, Engels and their Western followers had predicted that revolution would come first in those countries where capitalism was most advanced, because there the greatest contradiction between the forces and the relations of production would be found, as well as the largest, most sophisticated and most cheated working class. The disproof of international working class solidarity in 1914, combined with the outbreak of revolution in backward Russia were bad enough for European Marxists. Worse was that every attempt to further the revolutionary cause elsewhere miscarried. While the Bolsheviks explained their unexpected success with various *ad hoc* theories, such as Trotsky's 'law of uneven development', the cheated revolutionary intellectuals of the West turned back to the idealist sources of their thinking and that of Marx.

Marxism, conceived as a science of progressive historical development, shared the fate of those liberal bourgeois progressivisms whose naivety the Marxists had denounced. Belief in progress did not die in the First World War: what did perish was the common assumption that history itself could be trusted to deliver the goods. For the Marxists this meant a retreat from the determinist historical science of the theorists of the Second International and a new interest in cultural and ideological factors previously consigned, except by such eccentrics as George Sorel, to the periphery of investigation.

A major figure in this development was the Italian Communist leader Antonio Gramsci. He developed a theory of cultural hegemony, according to which the development of capitalism is accompanied by an ever denser ideological production. The theorists of the Second International believed that the deepening contradictions of capitalism would gradually undermine the credibility and coherence of the established order. This development would provide material for revolutionary theory and motive for revolutionary practice. It was expected to leave the ideological veil of capitalism looking very tattered. In contrast, Gramsci argued that, as the bourgeois system develops, those whom he called 'the organic intellectuals of the ruling class' produce ever more elaborate 'world views'. Against the threat of discovery a society based upon a lie throws up false views of reality. Good party man that he was, Gramsci solved this problem by developing the idea of a system of proletarian education as inclusive as that of the bourgeoisie. Bourgeois hegemony had to be answered by the hegemony of the proletariat, for only then would it be possible to develop a truly revolutionary consciousness. Gramsci did much of his writing in Mussolini's prisons and it is both ironic and suggestive of the fate of the Marxist idea that his reaction to the experience of totalitarianism was to propose a system at least as totalitarian as the one under which he suffered.

Gramsci's theory of hegemony was more sophisticated than previous Marxist discussions of the relationship between cultural experience, political consciousness and economic development. It was in Germany, however, and especially at the Frankfurt Institute of Social Research under the directorship of Horkheimer, that the new Western Marxist interest in cultural aspects of social reality was most fully developed. Horkheimer argued that revolutionary prospects were limited not only by the control of the bourgeoisie over culture but by a process of conditioning confirmed by every contact between the individual and his social environment. Materialist theory, as he then called it, could not confine itself to the analysis of movements in the economy. It must seek to understand the historical, cultural factors that conditioned people to accept things at their ideological face value. In his essay 'Authority and the Family', Horkheimer maintained

> If the direction and tempo of this process is ultimately determined by regularities within the economic apparatus of a society, yet the way in which men act at a given point in time cannot be explained solely by economic events which have transpired in the immediate past. It is rather the case that particular groups react according to the special character of their members and that this character has been formed in the course of earlier no less than of present social developments.[24]

Neither political activism nor economic analysis was enough: an inclusive hermeneutics of culture was needed, an interpretation, guided throughout by a predigested Marxist suspicion of established meaning-patterns as ideologically distorting. At certain moments in history the 'economic decline of a specific mode of production has so undermined all the cultural forms that go with it' that

> the needs of the greater part of society easily turn into rebellion and it takes only the resolute will of progressive groups to win the victory over the naked force of arms on which the whole system at this point essentially rests. But such moments are rare and brief: the decaying order is quickly improved where necessary and is apparently renewed; the periods of restoration last a long time, and during them the outmoded cultural apparatus as well as the psychic make-up of men and the body of interconnected institutions acquire new power.[25]

Horkheimer and his colleague Adorno became increasingly convinced that they were living in such a period of restoration. In his essay 'The Social Function of Philosophy', Horkheimer announced the theme which Marcuse later trumpeted around the world in his widely read *One Dimensional Man*: 'Technological progress has helped to make it even easier to cement old illusions more firmly and to introduce new ones into the minds of men without interference from reason.'[26] For this reason the traditional Marxist notion of consciously formed ideologies, analytically separable from social structure, was hopelessly outdated in industrial states. As Adorno put it:

> Today ideology means society as appearance. Although mediated by the totality behind which stands the rule of partiality, ideology is not simply reducible to a partial interest. It is, as it were, equally near the centre in all its pieces. . . . There are no more ideologies in the authentic sense of false consciousness, only advertisements for the world through its duplication and the provocative lie which does not seek belief but commands silence.[27]

Horkheimer and Adorno concluded that the human liberation that Marx had anticipated, the only possible justification for revolutionary politics, had become all but impossible. The very process of enlightenment which held up to man the mirror of free being, had also forged the chains that kept him from reaching through the looking glass. The domination of nature, which Marx like every child of the Enlightenment took to be the measure of man's autonomy, had become a new form of slavery to necessity. Drawing on Freud as much as on Marx, Horkheimer wrote in *Eclipse of Reason*: 'The human being, in the process of his emancipation, shares the fate of the rest of his world. Domination of nature involves domination of man. Every subject not only has to take part in the domination of external nature, human and non-human, but in order to do so must subjugate nature in himself.'[28] And while nature in man has always previously revolted against its own subjugation, 'Typical of our present era is the manipulation of this revolt by the prevailing forces of civilization itself, the use of revolt as a means of perpetuating the very conditions by which it is stirred up and against which it is directed. Civilization as rationalized irrationality integrates the revolt of nature as another means or instrument.'[29] Society as established lie, and established culture conceived as distortion and illusion are common Marxist themes, but the radical nature of Horkheimer's own version of this accusatory hermeneutics lies in his conclusion that the fault is not the function of any particular property arrangement or ideology of control but is ingrained in the nature of Reason itself. Speculative and practical reason, which are in Hegel and Marx respectively the agencies of progress, partake in the distorting process they can no longer transcend.

In his book, Horkheimer wrote:

> If one were to speak of a disease affecting reason, this disease should not be understood as having stricken at some historical moment, but as being inseparable from the nature of reason in civilization as we have known it so far. The disease of reason is that reason was born from man's urge to dominate nature, and the 'recovery' depends on insights into the nature of the original disease, not on a cure of its latest symptoms.[30]

Human enlightenment, in the form of instrumental rationality and technological effectiveness, freed man from the blind tyranny of natural forces only at the cost of subjecting him to the 'second Nature' of civilization. Society, like conquered nature, had become dominated by the operation of blind forces which the conditioned inmates were only too ready to interpret as unchangeable conditions of human existence. Technological progress might have raised man to a position in which he would be free to control his destiny in accord with the dictates of reason; in fact it had generated new forms of organization which trapped him in a second, social, realm of chance and necessity. The two processes, Horkheimer believed, were inextricably entwined in the process of enlightenment.

Nevertheless, at least in 1947, he did not consider the position hopeless:

> Advance in technical facilities for enlightenment is accompanied by a process of dehumanization. This process threatens to nullify the very goal it is supposed to realize . . . the idea of man. Whether the situation is a necessary phase in the general ascent of society as a whole, or

whether it will lead to a re-emergence of the neo-barbarism recently defeated on the battlefields, depends at least in part on our ability to interpret accurately the profound changes now taking place in the public mind and in human nature.[31]

The philosopher could help man to avoid his fate by showing him where he stood in the social and natural world. Reasonable control over the social world and respect for the natural were within his means yet the whole history of man's struggle against nature worked against their achievement in a rational social order.

The 'Critical Theory' of Horkheimer and Adorno was an attempt to realize this doubtful but desirable possibility by persuading men that the barriers to its attainment were man-made and therefore removable. Horkheimer saw this task as an extension of Marx's purpose in *Das Kapital:* to expose the supposedly natural laws of political economy as the ideological cloak of an outdated productive system. Horkheimer differed from Marx, and still more from the school of Kautsky, in rejecting the suggestion that history itself would reveal this fundamental truth and deliver man from the kingdom of necessity into the kingdom of freedom.

For Horkheimer and Adorno, Marx's equivocal position on this point showed him as the intellectual victim of his age and background. He had not emancipated himself from the nineteenth-century illusion of automatic progress and the Hegelian myth of the meaning of history. In a late essay on Schopenhauer, Horkheimer refers to 'the merciless structure of eternity'[32], while for his part Adorno insisted that 'No universal history leads from savagery to humanitarianism, but there is one leading from the slingshot to the megaton bomb.'[33] Arguing that Marx and Engels had failed to escape the idealist illusion that history embodies an immanent unfolding plan, Adorno claimed that they had therefore been blind to the importance of the individual and unique event. Further, they had built an automatic happy ending into their version of the historical drama when such an outcome was merely one possibility among many, and an unlikely one at that. Moved by wishful thinking and the belief that revolution was imminent, the founders of Marxism tended to picture liberation as a historically determined event. Rejecting the cold comfort of traditional ontology, they had made a metaphysics out of history, whose ways they sought to justify to the proletarian heirs of civilization. 'It was', says Adorno, 'a matter of deifying history, even to the atheistic Hegelians, Marx and Engels. The primacy of economics is to yield historically stringent reasons why the happy ending is immanent in history.'[34]

It is important that the Frankfurt theorists did not object to the image of free being which they found in Marx's early writings. Revolution implied liberation to precisely the extent that it permitted man to achieve the rational autonomy — revealed as his true nature and destiny by German idealism — in the conditions of his social existence. Horkheimer and his colleague agreed with Marx that this realization of freedom was only made possible by man's vastly increased productive powers. What they denied was that the connection was necessary or automatic. The liberation of man was, at best, a possibility at a historical moment when the conjunction of economic and cultural circumstances was right. That moment could pass unrecognized and leave behind it only the pathos of a promise unachieved. Increasingly in the course of their lives Horkheimer and Adorno were convinced that this had happened. Adorno held that Marx and Engels were never more Hegelian than when they were discussing history. Adorno's argument complemented Horkheimer's view that enlightenment was tragically tangled with the unthinking lust for dominance over nature. Though both men consistently rejected the claims of ontology and realist metaphysics, they admitted that such philosophies had at least the advantage of preserving a vestigial critical attitude toward the world of established fact, through the distinction between essence and appearance. In contrast, the rise of 'bourgeois' philosophy — in which they included the dominant strands of Western thinking since Descartes — and the rejection of metaphysics as a science of being distinct from the constitutive function of mind had driven the individual thinker back on the only datum he could still regard as certain, his own reason. In a wonderfully perceptive passage, Adorno identified the core problem of the philosophical tradition in which they all were rooted: 'Out of itself, the bourgeois *ratio* undertook to produce the order it had negated outside itself. Out of itself, however, that order ceased to be an order and was therefore insatiable. Every system was such an order, such an absurdly rational product: a posited thing posing as being-in-itself.'[25] In ways I shall suggest Adorno and Horkheimer too remained trapped in the idealist tradition but few thinkers have identified the illusion that lies at its heart as accurately as they.

The history of modern philosophy has been largely the history of competing inclusive systems. But, according to Adorno, each system reflects the individual thinker's class position and personal preferences rather than the nature of reality in itself. Consequently, his verdict on the Idealist masters was harsh. Idealism, he claimed, was an expression of rage against extra-mental reality. It reacted against it not so much because that reality was unjust as because it resisted the schematizing demands of individual reason. Instead of trying to comprehend the world, let alone to change it, Idealism attempted to force it into the neat categories of the mind. An imperialism of reason raised its frontier posts between man and the understanding of the world. 'To comprehend a thing in itself', wrote Adorno, 'not just to fit it in its system of reference, is nothing but to perceive the individual moment in its immanent connection with others.'[36] Idealism rejected the realist metaphysics of medieval and classical thinkers but constructed in its place a metaphysics of thinking. If the Aristotelians had too easily identified the content of their understanding with the reality of the universe, the Idealists had reduced that reality to a projection of mind. The result was a series of systems which, whatever their insights, always concluded by confining reality in a conceptual straitjacket.

Hegel's philosophy, with its dialectical logic, attempted to overcome this problem by stressing the contradictory character of the perceived world. Against the great tradition of Western philosophy Hegel stressed the centrality of conflict and contradiction. Adorno thought him correct in this but argued that even he had cut short the necessary work by capping his system with a self-resolving philosophy of history, one which integrated once again the recusant features of the real. Thus, his philosophy had become ideology and the understanding of reality its own disguise. Marx inherited from Hegel the concepts of conflict and contradiction but he transposed the level on which they operated from the history of thought and consciousness to that of economic history and social change. He also inherited the belief that these conflicts were self-resolving, something which, far from being implicit in the nature of events themselves, was really a form of the Idealist prejudice that the lines of reality follow the resolutions of the mind.

Marx's notion of natural laws of history was equivocal but, in *Negative Dialectics*, Adorno gave him the benefit of the doubt. He felt that Marx's talk of the natural laws governing capitalist society should not be taken literally; they were not to be understood as ontological laws of being. This interpretation was confirmed by what he took to be the 'strongest motive behind all Marxist theory: that these laws can be abolished.' 'The thesis that society is subject to natural laws is ideology if it is hypostatized as immutably given by nature. But this legality is real as a law of motion for the unconscious society, as *Das Kapital*, in a phenomenology of the anti-spirit, traces it from the analysis of the merchandise form to the theory of the collapse.'[37] Elsewhere, though, Adorno was less certain. He told Martin Jay in 1969: 'Marx wanted to turn the whole world into a giant workhouse.'[38]

Whatever the final verdict, Adorno and Horkheimer felt that a typically nineteenth century concern with impersonal historical processes and the *minutiae* of political economy had distracted Marx from developing the anti-ontological implications of his historical materialism. At times, it seemed that Marx had created a new Idealist system which differed from its precursors only in that its mental creations were disguised as men and social classes. This obscured the true position of man in capitalist society and furnished ideological justification for new systems of oppression which operated in its name. What the later political writings of Hegel had done for the Prussian monarchy, 'dialectical materialism' now did for Bolshevik dictatorship. In both cases ideology imposed an illusion of harmony over the discordant tragedy of the world.

Horkheimer and Adorno believed their own 'critical theory' was true to the insights of materialism, insights that Marx in his effort to decipher the course of history had reburied almost as soon as they had been attained. Horkheimer argued that attacks on materialism in its Marxist form are misdirected against 'the materialist thesis on the nature of total reality', the view that matter alone exists.[39] Engels in particular went astray when he argued in his philosophy of nature that matter was first being.

> In most non-materialist kinds of thought, [writes Horkheimer] insights become more meaningful and have greater implications as they become more general, comprehensive, and definitive statements of principle. It cannot be said that for the materialist the exact opposite is true (this would be the case only in extreme and therefore metaphysical nominalism). But it is true that the measure in which general points of view become decisive for action depends on the agent's concrete situation at any given moment. The attack upon one or another general philosophical thesis as supposedly decisive for the materialist's behaviour thus fails to grasp the real nature of materialist thought.

However, Horkheimer continues: 'Principle . . . can be of very great importance to the materialist too, but the reason for this is not to be found in the nature of the principle as such. The importance arises not from the theory alone but from the tasks which at any given period are to be mastered with the help of the theory.'[40] This pragmatic streak led Horkheimer eventually to describe his theory as 'critical' rather than 'materialist', because he felt that the latter term carried too much metaphysical baggage in its train with shades of Feuerbach and Epicurus. Critical theory was 'a theory dominated at every turn by a concern for reasonable conditions of life.'[41] The critical theorists' overwhelming concern with social matters he explained by the fact that 'The wretchedness of our own day is connected with the structure of society; social theory therefore forms the main content of contemporary materialism.'[42]

From Hegel and Marx the critical theorists developed their view of reality as riven by inescapable contradiction. More philosophically radical than their predecessors, they accused them of suppressing this permanent truth in a theory of history which looked to the historical process to resolve the irresolvable. The grand Marxist and Hegelian philosophies of history expressed not the nature of reality, which resisted all attempts to harmonize its discordant tones, but the ambition of the human mind to encapsulate its elements within the only terms it could fully encompass, the terms of identity and harmony. If their own dialectical thinking was difficult, this was — claimed the Frankfurt masters — the measure of the extent to which it was true to its object, 'even where the object does not heed the rules of thinking.'[43] Adorno affirmed that every ontology and every idealist system was the result of the unwillingness of consciousness to admit that reality was ultimately contradictory, and that, therefore, each was blind to what was truly objective in human experience, the joys and sufferings of the individual in the world.

The Frankfurt school levelled at Marx and Engels the criticism which had been levelled at the materialism of Feuerbach: in spite of appearances they had failed to make the final break with systematizing idealism and had therefore obscured the dissonant evidence of reality. Horkheimer and Adorno defended themselves against a similar charge by indicating how their own thought refuses to iron out contradictions for the sake of philosophical or psychological satisfaction. Every effort to comprehend the order of reality, whether it is conceived as an immutable order of being or an intelligible process of history, is dismissed by Adorno as a species of idealism, an imposition of the systematic categories of mind on the concrete irrationality of the real. The moment of truth is the fugitive instant of escape from rationalizing categories. This view which Adorno shares with Heidegger precludes the development of any rational ontology. If Heidegger is one of Adorno's most frequent critical targets it is not because he does not fully accept Heidegger's arguments against the metaphysical tradition. But rather because, in the thinking of the Frankfurt school, reason, not being, remains the *locus* of truth. Between Adorno and Heidegger there is agreement on the dissonance between rational discourse and experienced reality, but Adorno will never accept Heidegger's ontological identification of being, time and truth. Even if it were impossible to realize it, truth remains in the human dimension, image of a free future cast in the mould of liberating reason.

Is there not an idealist mortgage on the critical theorists' identification of ontology with the distortion of reality which they see as characteristic of idealism? Is every ontology an imposition on reality of subjective categories foreign to the object? Horkheimer and Adorno were the products of the post-Kantian thinking they criticized, and therefore, almost automatically, they accepted the position that knowable rational order must be a product of the subject and not the property of the object. This, combined with the Marxist and Nietzschian suspicion of philosophical reason, made them implacably hostile to the claims of ontology. They naturally identified metaphysics and ontology with subjectivism and idealism because, as post-Kantians, they could not accept intelligible order as anything but a product of the human mind. This is clear when Horkheimer declares:

> The major argument against ontology is that the principles man discovers in himself by meditation, the emancipating truths that he tries to find, cannot be those of society or of the universe, because neither of these is made in the image of man. Philosophical ontology is inevitably ideological because it tries to obscure the separation between man and nature and to uphold a theoretical harmony that is given the lie on every hand by the cries of the miserable and disinherited.[44]

There are four points to note in this passage: each draws attention to Horkheimer's debt to Idealist assumptions. In the first place he chooses to regard the principles of ontology as 'principles man discovers in himself'. If they were only that then metaphysical knowledge would only be a disguise put on by idealist speculation, and ontology could be dismissed as a psychology that has forgotten its own genesis. However, no one need feel bound to accept this position. In fact, it is only since the days of Kant and within the Idealist tradition that anyone has seriously maintained such a case. In considering its claims it is well to remember that Kant's theory was itself merely a response to the merciless analysis of David Hume which had, a generation before, shattered the causal assumptions of post-Cartesian rationalism and empiricism. As Gilson has pointed out, Kant's own case against the possibility of a metaphysical science, while overwhelmingly effective against the essentialist ontology of Christian Wolff, says nothing conclusive against the existentially based metaphysics of St Thomas Aquinas and his school.[45] Horkheimer, however, accepts as unquestionable the Kantian view that the human mind can only understand what it produces itself. Therefore, like Kant, he rejects the validity of metaphysics in advance. He takes as axiomatic for philosophy, as a whole and for ever, the solution given by one genius to the problems bequeathed by another's destruction of the coherence of the legacy of a third. It is not reality but the internal necessities of the debate between the ghosts of Kant, Hume and Descartes that force this supposed axiom on Horkheimer.

Secondly, Horkheimer declares that the principles that man finds within himself 'cannot be those of society or of the universe, because neither of these is made in the image of man.' Having accepted the Kantian rejection of the claims of metaphysics to discover an order of being in itself, he asserts that the human subject cannot find in his mind the principles governing extra-mental reality because that reality is not in fact formed in the image of mind. It is odd that a philosopher who emphasized the importance of restoring a proper understanding of the relationship between man and non-human reality should accept so uncritically the view that everything that is not mind-made is therefore unintelligible. If this were so, it might be best to destroy the darkling area or at least so subdue it that it bore at every level the imprint of man. But this was the attitude Horkheimer had identified as the flaw at the heart of the Enlightenment and human reason. Surely the respect for the complementary claims of the human and non-human world which is such a feature of the Frankfurt school implies a degree of understanding and a recognition of intelligible structure in nature. Furthermore, why, instead of imagining with the Idealist that the world is essentially the creature of mind, should we not consider the reverse proposition: that the mind is of its nature a dependent function of the very reality it is called upon to understand?

Then, Horkheimer rejects philosophical ontology as 'inevitably

ideological because it tries to obscure the separation between man and
nature and to uphold a theoretical harmony that is given the lie on every
hand by the cries of the miserable and disinherited.' There are two points
here. First, the attempt to trace an intelligible relationship between man
and cosmos is in no sense an attempt to obscure the distinctions involved.
Jacques Maritain's *The Degrees of Knowledge*, perhaps the most power-
ful and ambitious metaphysical treatise to appear this century, is subtitled: 'Distinguish to unite'[46]. Maritain's attempt to investigate the existence of a community of being that encompasses the human, the natural
and the supernatural, is explicitly founded upon the operations of a distinguishing, analytical intelligence which first investigates, as far as
possible, the nature and necessary conditions of each component within
the whole. Only when we have identified these distinct natures are we
ready to work out the necessary relationships that exist between them.
Again, Horkheimer reveals his imprisonment within the Idealist tradition, when he suggests that no intelligible link can be established between
man and his environment unless their respective identities are obscured.
   Finally, Horkheimer claims that any theoretical harmony which ontology claims to establish is denied by 'the cries of the miserable and
disinherited'. In other words, human suffering gives the lie to any supposed metaphysical order. This claim is levelled not only against
traditional ontologies but also against the metaphysics of Process or
History which the Frankfurt masters claimed to detect in Hegel and Marx.
A historicist ontology of the latter type usually justifies itself by appealing
to 'historical necessity', 'Progress' or some such phrase, while the meta-
physician of being normally treats suffering either as accidental to the
order of the real or necessary to it. Maritain took the second, more
unpopular course when he wrote in *Three Reformers*:

> The purely human order, the order of pure reason, is a harsh order, true
> and just, salutary and necessary, preserving Being, but bloodstained.
> Everywhere — under penalty of an infinitely harsher disorder — it
> involves limitation, constraint, the yoke, sacrifice to the good of the
> species or the common good. The executioner is a necessity for this
> order. The order of charity does not destroy it: it confirms it; but it
> perfects it supernaturally and without detriment to justice, imbues it
> with kindness. Then all is transfigured and renewed, every limitation
> turned to fullness, every sacrifice into love.[47]

This, I suppose, is the sort of passage that Horkheimer had in mind when
he wrote: 'I do not know how far metaphysicians are correct; perhaps there
is a particularly compelling metaphysical system or fragment. But I do
know that metaphysicians are usually impressed only to the smallest
degree by what men suffer.'[48]
   One can sympathize with Horkheimer's feelings without accepting

them as a reason for rejecting metaphysics. Ontological order is not necessarily moral order and the intelligible may be shocking, as the truth is sometimes painful. If we accept that the human mind is a function of the real and is capable of drawing the principles that guide its reason from its real object, then it is possible that however satisfying these principles are to the intellect they will still be repugnant to moral sense. It is conceivable that there is an intelligible objective order of being which is either empty of any governing moral principle or whose moral principle cannot be comprehended. The first is a classic position in Greek thinking and the second the view taken by traditional Christian thought. When Horkheimer rejects ontology on the grounds that the structure of being is not justifiable in personal moral terms he shows, again, the extent to which critical theory was unable to escape its idealist origins, in this case Kantian moralism. Morality has no valid claim against metaphysics unless the possibility of objective ontology is dismissed from the outset. The preoccupation with theodicy, the justification of the ways of the Creator to the created, in a metaphysics such as that of Leibniz, is evidence of a rationalized and therefore withered metaphysical sense, one which cannot allow for the transcendent mystery that bounds the sphere of knowledge. Against such an ontology the arguments of Adorno and Horkheimer are well justified, for the proper dependence of the moral 'ought' upon the ontological 'is' has already been tacitly reversed. The suspicious hermeneutics which, at the level of sociology, understands the substance of established society to be pure distortion rightly judges the essence of this ontology to be an immoral morality. The question is whether either society or ontology inevitably take this form, or whether their forms may be read in order to discover a truth which is other than the dialectical opposite of what they appear and claim to be.

The radical nature of suspicion in the work of Horkheimer and Adorno precludes this possibility, and the historicist substitute for theodicy which marks both the determinism of other forms of Marxist thought and Lukács' attempt to develop an ontology of social being. The price of such integral suspicion is estrangement from reality and a despairing political quietism which a political policeman might accept without approving it. The very radicalism of critical theory in the hands of Horkheimer and Adorno ironically undermined their revolutionary commitment, pushed them into political quietism and even, in the case of Horkheimer, into a qualified approval of the established society of the West.

When the student revolutionaries of Frankfurt urged Horkheimer, as Rector of their university, to support their demands he refused. Adorno too stood aloof and a group of eager female revolutionaries reacted to his hostility by baring their breasts at the old man in an attempt to disrupt his lectures. 'When I made my theoretical model I could not have guessed that people would try to realize it with Molotov cocktails' was Adorno's reaction to the less playful excesses of the same revolutionary movement.[49] Horkheimer prefaced the 1968 reissue of a selection of his earlier essays with the words 'An open declaration that even a dubious democracy, for all its defects, is always better than the dictatorship which would inevitably result from a revolution today, seems to me necessary for the sake of truth.'[50]

The irony was that the German student Left, keen to destroy that 'dubious democracy', justified its actions by appealing to an analysis of capitalist society largely the work of the Frankfurt Marxists. Rejected by their resident prophets, the German students turned to Marcuse for advice and inspiration. Alone among the triumvirate of philosophers who had given the school its distinctive character, Marcuse found his revolutionary hopes renewed by the experience of student revolutionary movement. Horkheimer, in contrast, warned that:

> to protect, preserve, and where possible, extend the limited and ephemeral freedom of the individual in the fact of the growing threat to it is far more urgent a task than to issue abstract denunciations of it or to endanger it by actions that have no chance of success. . . . Despite its dangerous potential, despite all the injustice that marks its course both at home and abroad, the free world is at the moment still an island in space and time, and its destruction in the ocean of rule by violence would also mean the destruction of the culture of which the critical theory is a part.[51]

We can partly explain the later political positions of Horkheimer and Adorno by reference to the horror of violence natural in those who had seen the rise of Nazism. It is impossible to read the passage in *Negative Dialectics* where Adorno meditates on the significance of Auschwitz without sensing the darkness of the shadow cast by the extermination camps. Most of the leading figures of the Frankfurt school were Jewish, and, before the war, in common with most assimilated German Jews, they had minimized the significance of any specific 'Jewish Problem'. Franz Neuemann, also associated with the Frankfurt Institute, believed that the Germans were the least anti-semitic nation in Europe. After the war all was changed and in the writings of the half-Jewish Adorno in particular the horror of the mass murder of European Jewry is vividly present. Having once written that 'to write poetry after Auschwitz is barbaric', he later changed his mind, stating:

> Perennial suffering has as much right to expression as a tortured man has to scream; hence it may have been wrong to say that after Auschwitz you could no longer write poems. But it is not wrong to raise the less cultural question whether after Auschwitz you can go on living — especially whether one who escaped by accident, one who by rights should have been killed, may go on living. His mere survival calls for

the coldness, the basic principle of bourgeois subjectivity, without which there could have been no Auschwitz; this is the drastic guilt of him who was spared. By way of atonement he will be plagued by dreams such as that he is no longer living at all, that he was sent to the ovens in 1944 and his whole existence since has been imaginary, an emanation of the insane wish of a man killed twenty years earlier.[52]

This passage alone illuminates the tragic dimension of Adorno's and Horkheimer's abandonment of revolutionary faith. They had seen too much to dismiss Ernst Bloch's words: 'Hidden in the *citoyen* was the bourgeois; may God have mercy on us for what hides in the comrade.'[53]

Yet, though this factor is important, it is not the crucial determinant of their gradual retreat from revolutionary commitment. At the risk of seeming perverse, it is possible to interpret the development as a function of the radicalism of their suspicion of established reality. Where actuality is read as a fundamental distortion of potential, and historicism is rejected as a consoling hope, the link between thought and action becomes tenuous and may break. Thought clings to a possibility which it now recognizes as nearly unattainable, while action continues, as it must, in the world as it is. This is the tension manifested in Horkheimer's rejection of his intellectual progeny. The Utopian vision which continued to govern the action of young enthusiasts had been banished from the range of possibility entertained by their masters. Others within the Marxist tradition have interpreted the Frankfurt theorists' estrangement of theory from practice as a function of their lack of direct involvement in political struggle and their highly abstract philosophical interests. In contrast, I believe that the writings of Horkheimer and Adorno reveal tensions that are latent in the whole Marxist conception of social reality. For a moment, in their works, the metastatic project of Marxism became conscious of its futility in a world it does not recognize as ultimately real but which obstinately refuses to disappear. This development, in turn, may be read as the working out of the ultimate consequences of an idealist tradition that refuses, against all the evidence, to recognize the ontological priority of supra-human being over consciousness.

Idealism expresses suspicion of the world, by refusing to accept experienced reality as a field ultimately not dependent upon ourselves. Certainly we can destroy ourselves and the world in which we live: what we cannot do is to create a new cosmos out of the chaos that would result. That the world, and our necessary ways of being in it, may not be to our taste is a poor guide to action when action itself is not recognized as taking place within a limited space that is ours to cultivate and enjoy.

A brief sketch of the genesis of Frankfurt Marxism, the reasons for its estrangement from revolutionary practice and, more broadly, the way in which its fate shows up the inadequacy of Marxist thought in general are in place. The Marxist tradition is, as I have shown, an off-shoot of German idealist philosophy. Despite debts to earlier rationalism, it is rooted in the experience of Lutheran Protestant thinkers and thereby in the ferment of the Reformation and its reformulation of Christian truth. We can trace a line from Luther to the Frankfurt school which passes through Kant, Hegel, Marx and a host of less influential thinkers. This line can be seen as a historical record of the fate of that radical dissatisfaction with worldly order which was one of the legacies of the Protestant reformers. The systems of the various philosophers along the way represent successive attempts to overcome the resultant tension in existence, either by distinguishing man absolutely from his surroundings, or by conceiving them as the product of his mind or labour.

In viewing the world as irremediably fallen and human reason as a misleading whore of the Devil, Luther set up a tension which has not yet been relieved. In following the nominalistic currents of his time and rejecting the claims of natural theology and metaphysics, he prefigured in a theological scheme Kant's distinction between the impure world of phenomena and the epistemologically untouched and cognitively untouchable noumenal world of things-in-themselves. Depriving man of the possibility of even limited metaphysical knowledge of the nature of reality, Kant left him still conscious of the unattainable. His dissident disciple, Fichte, resolved the problem by dispensing with the independent universe of things-in-themselves — but at the cost of an absolute idealism which conceived extra-mental reality as the product of the thinking subject. Hegel, more subtly, overcame the Kantian dichotomy by historicizing the picture. He argued that the tensions and contradictions which do indeed exist at present can only be overcome if the distinction between knowing subject and known object is itself overcome. This is precisely what History signifies when it is conceived as the process by which God or Reason or the World Spirit (the terms are almost interchangeable) comes to recognize Himself in the world He has created.

By the time of Marx the initial problem — whether the human mind attains true knowledge of the order of being or not — had been obscured. The question was: what must be done in order to further this progressive self-consciousness by bringing the conditions of human life into accord with what we conceive to be man's potential? Marx's Young Hegelian friends took for granted that man was the seat of that self-consciousness which Hegel had identified with the World Spirit. Marx very practically pointed out that the rearrangement of the conditions of human life would never be accomplished by thought alone. The constraints were material, economic and political, and Revolution alone could accomplish the ambition of philosophy to achieve self-conscious freedom in a man-made world.

If one asks how we are to arrive at human fulfilment without asking about the nature of man and his relationship to the surrounding universe, or if, like Marx, one sees this nature and relationship as ever changing, one is likely to arrive at a position of optimism rooted in a Utopian vision of an impossible autonomy and freedom. When later disappointments turn up along the way, disappointments which arise in the failure of one's successes to bring about the imagined results, one may succumb to the belief that human history is dogged by an immanent evil demon. Horkheimer and Adorno found their demon in human enlightenment itself. They argued powerfully that by the use of reason man had conquered Nature and suppressed her fire in himself. The prison he had erected for himself, the social structures founded on his new dominance over nature, had become a new shrine of irrationality all the worse in that it was built in the name of reason. Man had built his own prison walls.

Enlightenment man, who broke the bonds of religion and metaphysics, had proved to be the architect of a new and possibly cataclysmic fate. Critical theory strove to teach him before it was too late that he had the power and knowledge to organize his life in accordance with the dictates of reason on the human scale. Yet it said nothing of the limitations he would have to accept to prevent the same disastrous process repeating itself at a later and more dangerous date. Instead, it specifically approved the idealist doctrine that all such limitations are historically relative and therefore potentially transcendable. Horkheimer felt there was a kinship between materialism and metaphysical pessimism, yet his view of the possible future of man was not only optimistic but, in view of his awareness of the double-edged significance of enlightenment, quite fantastic. Perhaps this recognition led the old master of suspicion to his peaceful retirement in Switzerland, grudgingly grateful that he would live out his days in peace before the deluge. Marcuse might lead the chorus of liberation but his colleagues' fighting days were over.

7 Aspects of Realism

What is realism? What does a realistic approach to the human sciences involve? These questions posed themselves with increasing urgency when we turned from the development of the ideas of such men as Voegelin, Ricoeur, Jonas, Schutz and Vivas to the alternative currents of thought represented by the positivists and the Marxists. Positivism unjustifiably narrows the range of science and is consequently insensitive to aspects of reality implied by but not contained in events in the external world. Marxism is a species of covert idealism, a theory that fails, despite its explicit pretensions, to bring the insights of idealism back to earth, and therefore to take account of man and his context as they really are. One issue of particular contrast between the Marxist approach and that espoused here is that of the relationship between human nature and social organization. Realism in the human sciences focuses upon the historically and archaeologically warranted assumption that a relatively stable human nature exists which combines aggressive and cooperative elements, and that political orders, in all their variety, reflect the nature of the human animal who makes them up. In Marxism this position is significantly reversed.

It is possible for the realist to alternate between an Aristotelian view of man as a political animal whose communal life reflects a capacity for friendship, and a Hobbesian conception of society as a collective defence against the antisocial and murderous side of human nature. The realist cannot accept Marx's assumption that human nature is only a reflection of the social arrangements made by men themselves, and that men will one day achieve a near Utopian existence under communism because the socio-economic arrangements will then prevent the rise of new patterns of domination. Marx expresses this principle in the sixth of the *Theses on Feuerbach:* 'Human nature is no abstraction inherent in each separate individual. In its reality it is the ensemble of social arrangements.' The French Marxist, Louis Althusser, regards this as the *locus* of what he calls the 'epistemological break' between Marxist science and the merely ideological theories of Marx's predecessors. Althusser is right to see the point as crucial, though I see its significance in a different light.

The principle of the sixth *Thesis,* which makes of human nature a product of social arrangements and explicitly rejects an ontologically prior human nature actualized in man's social existence, makes it possible for Utopian speculation on the future of man to mask itself as science. The realist does not deny that different social arrangements encourage the various typical characteristics of man, but he maintains that these characteristics are coeternal with human existence and none can be exhausted or transcended. In so far as political order embodies both the given nature and the creative activity of man, social and political systems are more or less satisfactory variations on themes as old as Adam.

This is not all there is to realism, even of the common-sense variety. When Sartre declared, in *Existentialism and Humanism* (1948): 'We are precisely in a situation where there are only human beings', Heidegger retorted; 'We are precisely in a situation where principally there is Being.'[1] One need not be a follower of Heidegger to acknowledge the weight this reply must carry for the realist. Human nature is a central concept for realism but its significance cannot be understood in isolation from the environmental context. Reality, as a process experienced by man in the space of the cosmos and the time of history, is a lesson in modesty, an intensive course in the meaning of finitude and contingency. This point was expressed poignantly by Albert Camus in *The Rebel*[2]. There Camus vividly portrays what happens when the human impulse to rebel against a situation perceived to be unjust becomes confused with the illusion of human infinity and the myth of the total transformation of the world. Metaphysical rebellion, Camus argues, is the hard centre of the cult of revolution. It involves the blurring and eventual dissolution of the distinction between what is man-made and can be changed and what is not. Camus' atheism, a very Mediterranean paganism of place and fate, is different from that of Marx or Feuerbach. They substitute man for God as world creator, while Camus reawakens us to the pre-existing reality in which we live and die and which sets the limits of achievement. At worst men must try to make the best of a bad job. At best the achievements of the human spirit are there for all to see.

Camus is less an atheist than a pagan humanist, whose soul is suffused with a sense of absolute dependence on transcendent reality. This, because it is the authentic sense of the real, permits feelings of pride as well as shame before the works of man. Where that sense is lost, no independent measure for man and no way of distinguishing the objectively real from the subjectively desired exists. Camus' testament retains particular importance, coming from a confessed atheist and man of the political Left. He was a natural rebel who detested even the minor injustices inseparable from social life, but understood the climax of totalitarianism implicit in the rejection of the ontological level that is man's lot within reality.

Camus should be read by students of Marxist ideas, because it is to the sense of injustice and the feeling for mundane perfection that these ideas make their first and often compelling appeal. Even as the appeal is made we must be clear about the point from which it sounds. Is the call to revolution aimed at the achievement of a goal we could reasonably hope to attain, or is it a cry from Utopia? Is the torrent of suspicion and condemnation loosed upon established order a cleansing wave, or does it flow from a judgement of what is by the standards of what can never be? The solution to real problems can only be found in reality itself. The Utopian must always hide from himself and others the ontological chasm between intention and achievement. Thus what purports to be a road to freedom leads into deception and deprivation. The Utopian justifies his actions with false science, he may destroy the social and political institutions which he imagines to stand in his way, but the problem remains. At that stage he must turn from destroying particular institutions, social groups and individuals, to suppressing reality itself. Though reality cannot be suppressed on the level of existence, for things remain as they are, it can be suppressed at the level of consciousness through the propagation and enforcement of a total ideology which distorts the evidence of reality. With this, as its last resort and only guarantee, must come the silencing of anyone who sees through the veil.

One should not disguise the difficulties that attend the use of the terms 'reality', 'the real' and 'realism'. 'Realism' and the 'real', deployed as terms in argument, take colour from what they are opposed to. This includes a tone of systemic dogmatism that is foreign to the experience to which the terms answer. 'Realism,' in the medieval sense, as opposed to nominalism, is not identical in range or content with 'realism' as a modern term for anti-idealist ways of thinking. Yet neither are the two contradictory as Popper has suggested. 'Realism' is the term I use to evoke the exploration of what asserts itself in experience however we try to banish it from consciousness. It has an anti-idealist and an anti-nominalist aspect. Realism is not a system nor a doctrine but a sense, or a sensitivity. It is essentially a sense of contingency to and participation in a community of being which looks to us neither for its initial existence nor for its defining character. This implies relationship, not autonomy. The conceptual abstraction as well as the completeness of the grand idealist systems are absent from realist thinking. Alien to it also is the conventionalism implied in nominalist accounts of language, and especially the ontological language of natures and essences.

The integral realist conceives of reality as he experiences it: a reality of natures or types, in which man inter-relates with other types of being no less finite than himself. All participate in a process whose beginning and end are unknown, which men comprehend through creating symbols that render intelligible the discovered problems and mysteries of existence. Yet, in opposing idealism, which reverses the relationship between finite consciousness and transcendent being, we cannot pretend that mind merely mirrors the world; and in opposing nominalism, which reduces our knowledge of essence to a process of pragmatically motivated labelling, we must acknowledge that reality does not speak its own truth but requires the mediation of human language with all the emergent novelty that implies. There are problems in expressing the relationship of consciousness and language, within the real — problems realism cannot avoid. Deepest of these is that talk of reality makes an apparently discrete object of that process in which it is an event. We are part of what we speak when we say 'reality'.

In this chapter I shall examine these problems drawing on the work of Voegelin whose investigations in the field are unsurpassed. His theory of consciousness and symbolization and his investigation of the particular symbols 'reality' and 'being' have already played a large part in the argument. Then I shall consider what the investigation implies for the conception of interpretation and explanation in the sciences of man. In the space seen through the mesh of creation and discovery in symbolization the figure of true realism is found.

One of Voegelin's recent statements on the analysis of consciousness comes from a summary of his intellectual development written to introduce Gerhart Niemeyer's translation of his book *Anamnesis*. Voegelin was dissatisfied with what he saw as an unjustifiable restriction of the horizon of consciousness both in the dominant academic philosophies of the time and the ideological mass movements:

> I had observed the restriction, and recognized it as such, with the criteria of the observation coming from a consciousness with a larger horizon, which in this case happened to be my own. And if that was true, then the school-construction of an 'intersubjective' ego as the subject of cognition did not apply to an analysis of consciousness; for the truth of my observation did not depend on the proper functioning of a 'subject of cognition' in the Kantian, or neo-Kantian, sense when confronted with certain 'subjective' deformations. An analysis of consciousness, I had to conclude, has no instrument other than the concrete consciousness of the analyst. The quality of this instrument, then, and consequently the quality of the results, will depend on what I have called the horizon of consciousness; and the quality of the horizon will depend on the analyst's willingness to reach out into all the dimensions of the reality in which his conscious existence is an event, it will depend on his desire to know. A consciousness of this kind is not an a priori structure, nor does it just happen, nor is its horizon a given, it rather is a ceaseless action of expanding, ordering, articulating, and correcting itself; it is an event in the reality of which as a part it partakes. It is a permanent effort at responsive openness to the appeal of reality, at bewaring of premature satisfaction, and above all at avoiding the self-destructive phantasy of believing the reality of which it is a part to be an object external to itself that can be mastered by bringing it into the form of a system.[3]

He is describing the process which he has termed the 'opening of the soul', in which the philosophical man becomes conscious of his soul as a 'sensorium of transcendence', a register of the real as it emerges from and shades into the mystery of the beginning and the beyond, and of the intimations of the transcendent source of that process which men call God. Consciousness responds to reality of which it is a part and in which its response is an event:

> By virtue of their consciousness . . . human beings are quite conscious of being parts of a comprehensive reality and express their awareness by the symbols of birth and death, of a cosmic whole structured by realms of being, of a world of external objects and of the presence of divine reality in the cosmos, of mortality and immortality, of creation into the cosmic order and of salvation from its disorder, of descent into the depth of the *psyche* and meditative ascent toward its beyond. Within this rich field of reality-consciousness . . . there occur the processes of wondering, questing, and seeking, of being moved and drawn into the search by a consciousness of ignorance, which, in order to be sensed as ignorance, requires an apprehension of something worth to be known; of an appeal to which man can lovingly respond or not so lovingly deny himself: of the joy of finding truth from the compact to differentiated experiences and symbols; and of the great breakthrough of insight through visions of the prophetic, the philosophic, and the Christian-apostolic type. In brief, Man's conscious existence is an event within reality, and man's consciousness is quite conscious of being constituted by the reality of which it is conscious. The intentionality is a substructure within the comprehensive consciousness of a reality that becomes luminous for its truth in the consciousness of man.[4]

This response of consciousness is not to be misconstrued in a mechanistic sense. The mode of human response is symbolic. To speak of symbols is to speak of human works, that primarily articulate reality but may, when separated from the experience that engenders them, stand as a screen between man and the real. The phenomenon of the loss of reality finds its source in this, and it is the clue to the distorting nature of ideology. Voegelin's method is always to trace engendered symbols to engendering experience, yet, as he admits, these are not easily distinguished. Language and experience cannot be treated as independent entities, for experience is known only as articulated in symbols which, in turn, are modified,

> in order to let the truth of symbols more adequately render the truth of reality experienced. The truth of consciousness, its verification and advance, could not be identified with either the truth of statements or the truth of experience; it was a process that let its truth become

luminous in the procedural tension between experience and symbolization. Neither the experiences nor the symbols could become autonomous objects of investigation for an outside observer. The truth of consciousness revealed itself through participation in the process of reality; it was essentially historical.[5]

These considerations have determined Voegelin's work of the last thirty or so years. His explorations take the form of a historical and philosophical hermeneutics which, guided by the classical desire to pursue ontological truth, analyses those symbols through which men in history have articulated their experience. This accounts both for the range of Voegelin's interests, and the formative unity of the whole opus. The interest in symbolization is not merely academic: it is a human desire to understand the reality of which the symbols more or less obliquely speak. As such, it illuminates the nature of the human sciences whose realm is constituted by the existence of a level of phenomena already created by man in his effort to come to terms with his being. In every part of the field, from literary criticism to sociology, one is concerned with interpreting an achieved level of intentional activity that occurs within a pre-existing and fundamentally limiting framework of reality. The nature of this framework is disclosed only gradually through ongoing experience, and then never completely. We act on a stage whose boundaries we do not know except to say that they are not limitless. The knowledge we gain is the product of careful interpretation of the positions in which we find ourselves, and the clue to these is in the reactions they give rise to.

In an essay published in 1970, 'Equivalences of Experience and Symbolization in History', Voegelin has usefully summarized his theory of symbolization in seven propositions:

1 Man participates in the process of reality. The implications of the fundamental proposition, then, can be expressed by the following propositions:
2 Man is conscious of reality as a process, of himself as being part of reality, and of his consciousness as a mode of participation in its process.
3 While consciously participating, man is able to engender symbols which express his experience of reality, of himself as the experiencing agent, and of his conscious experiencing as the action and passion of participating.
4 Man knows the symbols engendered to be part of the reality they symbolize — the symbols consciousness, experience, and symbolization denote the area where the process of reality becomes luminous to itself. To the positive statements we ... can add three corollaries of a cautionary nature:
5 Reality is not a given that could be observed from a vantage point

outside itself but embraces the consciousness in which it becomes luminous.

6 The experience of reality cannot be total but has the character of a perspective.

7 The knowledge of reality conveyed by the symbols can never become a final possession of truth, for the luminous perspective that we call experiences, as well as the symbols engendered by them, are part of reality in process[6]

These seven propositions assist the understanding of Voegelin's approach to reality and suggest a path which I believe the sciences of man would do well to follow.

Authoritatively, Voegelin has set down the cognitive consequences of man's ontological position in the order of being. In particular, he warns us against separating thought from experience, or attributing to symbols an autonomy and a finality they do not possess. Knowledge is always provisional: what is constant is the structure of existence to which human symbolic activity responds. Yet the emergent novelty of symbols, a precondition for their exploratory potential, is also, when divorced from experience, a source of illusion and distortion. A true symbol articulates the experience of a soul open to transcendent reality, and, once engendered, must not inhibit the further flow of reality. Metaphor is a case in point. A metaphor is a cognitive instrument that permits its creator and his audience to understand something previously unrecognized which perhaps could not have been seen without it. But when a metaphor is treated as an acquired truth it ceases to enlighten and becomes a weapon of obfuscation. The history of social and political thought abundantly exemplifies the consequences of taking literally the genuinely enlightening analogy between society and the organism. Even great historical thinkers have sometimes wasted their efforts in trying to show, for instance, that civilizations have a natural cycle of life and death equivalent to that of the body. Spengler and Toynbee are vivid examples.

There is a more important point about the relative independence of achieved symbols from engendering experience: the problem of error which, when systematically pursued in a refusal to attend to the evidence of the real, leads to the phenomenon Voegelin calls 'The Eclipse of Reality'.[7] In his essay of that title he delineates the result of man's refusal to accept the conditions of his participation in being, when he ceases to acknowledge the intelligible links between himself and his context. Using the typical vocabulary of Jean-Paul Sartre, Voegelin diagnoses the phenomena of ideology and ideologically contracted man, and throws considerable light on the necessary complexities of the term 'reality.'

By an act of imagination, [Voegelin writes] man can shrink himself to a self that is 'condemned to be free'. To this shrunken or contracted self . . . God is dead, the past is dead, the present is the flight from the self's non-essential facticity towards being what is not, the future is the field of possibles among which the self must choose its project of being beyond mere facticity, and freedom is the necessity of making a choice that will determine the self's own being.

Modern man is typically characterized by such contraction and modern ideological thought is structured by the need to live with this contraction and make it bearable. The peculiar character of the consequent task is obvious when we recall that it is only man's consciousness of himself as a participant in the community of being that makes reality meaningful to him. Inevitably, then, the satisfaction of the needs of the contracted self will involve a distortion of reality:

> As neither the man who engages in deforming himself to a self ceases to be a man; nor the surrounding reality of God and man, world and society does change its structure; nor the relations between man and his surrounding reality can be abolished; frictions between the shrunken self and reality are bound to develop. The man who suffers from the disease of contraction, however, is not inclined to leave the prison of his selfhood, in order to remove the frictions. He rather will put his imagination to further work and surround the imaginary self with an imaginary reality apt to confirm the self in its pretence of reality; he will create a Second Reality . . . in order to screen the First Reality of common experience from his view. The frictions consequently, far from being removed, will grow into a general conflict between the world of his imagination and the real world. . . . A reality projected by imagination . . . is not the reality of common experience. Nevertheless, a man's act of deforming himself is as real as the man who commits it, and his act of projecting a Second Reality is as real as the First Reality it intends to hide from view. The imaginator, his act of imagination, and the effects the act has on himself as well as on other people, thus, can claim to be real. Some imaginative constructions of history, designed to shield the contracted self, as for instance those of Comte, or Hegel, or Marx, even have grown into social forces of such strength that their conflicts with reality form a substantial part of global politics in our time. The man with a contracted self is as much of a power in society and history as an ordinary man, and sometimes a stronger one. The conflict *with* reality turns out to be a disturbance *within* reality.[8]

When William Croft, at the end of the seventeenth century, set the Anglican funeral service to music, he kept the verses beginning, 'Thou knowest Lord . . .' in the setting of Henry Purcell, on the grounds that no one could set them better. That is how I see Voegelin's analysis of the eclipse of reality. It goes to the heart of the problem of the relationship between the imagined universes of ideological thought and the reality of the universe of common experience. Contraction to a self amounts to a loss of the ontological dimension. It means, as idealist philosophical systems show, the rejection of a knowable order inherent in but prior to experience. It results too in the dichotomy of the fact/value distinction in modern philosophy, which a priori precludes the attainment of an objective theory of ethical or political good. The defence of the contracted self, philosophically exemplified in academic constructions from Descartes's Ego to Husserl's Transcendental Consciousness, requires the fantasy of another, imagined, order derived from the subject. This order is unrealistic, but not unreal in its consequences, for illusion is at least as strong a spur to action as truth, especially when the illusion requires the rearrangement or transformation of the elements of reality to fit the new requirements.

At one level it could be argued that Voegelin's philosophy undercuts the distinction between realism and idealism which I have been stressing. Certainly the distinction is unknown to the Greek philosophers whom Voegelin follows when he treats consciousness as the event in reality in which the truth of being emerges. And Voegelin's well-known dislike of all 'Isms', political and academic, arising from a suspicion of the intellectual limitations which they impose, would work against my usage. This is a matter of more than marginal importance. If the broad lines of Voegelin's approach are to be accepted, it would undermine my project of extending it to sociology if I were to start with a significant act of dissent.

Let me, then, explore the matter further. Voegelin's rejection of the Cartesian and Husserlian project of finding an absolute starting point for a philosophy of consciousness vindicates the common-sense claim that, in Paul Valéry's words: 'there is no theory that is not a fragment, carefully prepared, of some autobiography.'[9] Voegelin admires Thomas Reid, the Scots philosopher of common sense. To see the common-sense point of departure for his own argument we have only to consider his down-to-earth dismissal of one of the major problems in Husserl's phenomenology: how other subjects can be constituted in the consciousness of the ego. He wrote to Schutz in 1943:

> Husserl's great question, — How is the Thou consittuted in the I as an alter ego? — takes care of itself in that the Thou is not constituted in the I at all. The problem of the Thou seems to me to resemble that of all other classes of transcendence. The fact that consciousness has an experience of the other, as a consciousness of the other, is not *a problem* but a given of experience from which one may start out but behind which one may not retreat.[10]

In this reaction against Husserl, Voegelin leaves the Subject/Object framework dominant in Western thought since Descartes, and enters a problem area dominated by the desire to understand the way in which experienced reality achieves expression in various forms of discourse ranging from myth to theory. Voegelin's is a philosophy of the openness of consciousness to reality, and the openness of the reality of immediate experience to Divine transcendence. However, immediate cosmic experience does not speak its own truth; rather, it provokes man, through symbolic language, to develop terms adequate to its expression. The specific difference of the symbolism of philosophy is the careful differentiation that corresponds to a highly differentiated experience of reality.

> At the beginning of philosophy [Voegelin writes] there is the dissociation of a cosmos-full-of-gods into a dedivinized order of things and a divinity whose relations to the newly discovered character of the universe is still unclear. The Hellenic thinkers named that which revealed itself to their differentiating experience *being;* and ever since being has been for philosophers the subject of all propositions about order and nature.[11]

There is a problem here, which is no trivial puzzle but the mystery of the relationship between language and reality. It has proved a rich field for twentieth century thinkers. Consider what Voegelin is saying when he writes: 'The difficulties of expressing the philosophical experience adequately, and yet without derailing, roots in the fact that philosophizing about the non-objective field of the tensions of being is tied to a language the grammar of which depicts objective images of the world of things.'[12] To speak of something is to imply a distance between the speaker and the spoken, between subject and object, which allows the object to be seen as such. But between man and reality there is no such space. Furthermore, the distance from reality, covertly suggested by the subject, object framework, is inevitably present in the objectifying speech of philosophical discourse, though absent in immediate experience. Language exacts a price for the speaking of truth. Thus discourse about reality or being can only continue to convey the truth of experience if it remains aware of its misleading perspective. This it cannot easily do: it would involve saying that, on the one hand, A is the truth, and, on the other, that A is depicted falsely. However, what a discursive text does not do for itself can be done by the interpreter who continually questions back from the engendered symbols of speech to the engendering experience. This is what Voegelin does in his interpretations of classical and biblical texts.

We witness here the emerging outline of what Ricoeur has called 'the dialectic of understanding and explanation' in the procedures of the human sciences: 'the view that explanation and understanding would not constitute mutually exclusive poles, but rather relative moments in a complex process called interpretation.'[13] Our earlier failure to see matters in this way is partly a result of the notion of causal explanation left us by positivism, and of the polemical use of the terms explanation and understanding *(verstehen)* in debates about the methodology of social science. In Voegelin's work methodological considerations are properly subservient to questions of theoretical relevance and clarification; the dialectical relationship between understanding and explanation can therefore emerge. Interpretation, which questions back from engendered symbol to engendering experience, discovers an experience of reality which explains the origin of a certain pattern of symbols. A particular experience may provide the necessary condition for the development of a particular set of symbols, though the actual development is the work of the man who experiences. The relationship is, in a necessarily broad sense, causal, inso far as the experience sparks off the symbolization process, but the spark does not always light the fire and, once lit, the fire does not always spread in the one direction. This is a function of the free and creative dimension of consciousness, including its power to close itself to experienced reality, or to develop different or even opposed symbols to articulate the same experience. Thus the one experience of transcendence provokes both mythical symbols of gods and heroes and philosophical symbols of finitude within infinity.

In Voegelin's phrase, 'the non-objective field of the tensions of being', the term 'non-objective' does not imply that the field is subjective, in the sense that is is either constituted by the human subject or structured by him. 'There is no reality,' Voegelin writes, 'other than that of which we have consciousness',[14] and this is non-objective only in that it cannot, without distortion, be treated as an object of knowledge before or outside of which the subject stands. To speak of reality as other than the speaker or the speech in which its truth is articulated is misleading. But this is what the nature of language compels us to do. Speaker and speech are events in reality, never merely spectators or witnesses of it. What we experience, and what we convey of that experience, are parts of a process in which we participate. Such considerations preserve Voegelin from the narrow objectivism which pretends to capture the essence of the real in conceptual formulae claiming to embody truth once and for all. Voegelin's suspicion of metaphysical thinking when it takes the form of philosophical or religious doctrine is a further function of this. The preservation of experienced truth in timeless propositions is an intrinsically problematic undertaking. It is as though, having once bathed in a mountain stream, one tried to eternalize the experience by keeping bottles of stream water in the refrigerator for the occasional dab. Faced with the bottled concepts of philosophy the interpreter must analyse the content in order to trace the source, for there the ontological truth of experience is found.

Yet in rejecting rigid objectivism there is another peril to be avoided. Consider what happens when we say that reality cannot be an object for thinking man because it is not other than the thinker, the speaker or the language in which it is spoken. We are then tempted to treat what is or can be thought as coterminous with the real, and this is the trap of idealism and subjectivism. To avoid this we must bear in mind that though reality is not something apart from the speaker and the speech it is something infinitely more than them. Consciousness depends upon reality while reality, except as a symbol of speech, does not depend upon consciousness. Though I am but a moment in the whole, open to the experience of the process in which I effectively participate, the experience is of an open horizon extending into infinity. Schutz went to the heart of the matter as it emerges in mundane experience when he wrote: 'the world within my actual reach carries along the open infinite horizons of my world in potential reach, but to my experiences of these horizons belongs the conviction that each world within potential reach, once transformed into actual reach, will again be surrounded by new horizons, and so on.'[15]

In Voegelin's view the 'open, infinite horizon' of experience implies that a philosophy which wishes to take account of this constitutive feature of man's being, as a true philosophy must do, will recognize the validity of the symbols of God and the Divine. They articulate an awareness of ultimate transcendence, of a Being transcending the cosmos, whose source of order and being He is. Voegelin wrote to Schutz:

> I incline to believe that the process theological attempt and its expansion, a metaphysics that interprets the transcendence system of the world as the immanent process of a divine substance, is the only meaningful systematic philosophy. It at least tries to interpret the world order transcending consciousness in a 'comprehensible' language, while any ontologically different metaphysic not only cannot comprehend transcendence in immanence but also adds the nonsense of interpreting it in a language that is 'incomprehensible' because it is not oriented to the only experience of consciousness which is accessible 'from within'.[16]

We are now talking of reality as a process emerging from and projecting into a mysterious realm evoked by the symbols of the Divinity, the Beginning and the Beyond. As we noted, philosophy attempts in its own self-conscious way to make sense of the same mystery of reality as transcending experience to which myths of supernatural origin and destiny have everywhere answered. The philosophical quest for the *arche* or origin of things recasts in philosophical terms the question pre-philosophically answered by the cosmogonic myth. We witness the emergence of a distinctly philosophical approach in a text which has delineated the cognitive space of philosophy ever since, Anaximander's dictum (A 9;B1): 'The origin *(arche)* of things is the Unbounded *(apeiron)*. . . . It is necessary for things to perish into that from which they were born; for they pay one another penalty for their injustice *(adikia)* according to the ordinance of Time.' Here, in compact form, is the authentically philosophical experience of the finite status of things and of knowledge, in short, of limitation. Anaximander's *Apeiron*, the symbol of the infinite or unbounded which is truly sayable only in so far as we do not try to bind it by definition, raises the question of the source and the end of experienced reality in a way genuinely novel in the history of consciousness. Before Anaximander there are on the one hand, narratives of the gods and, on the other, the physicalistic answer of Thales who believed water to be the origin of all. In comparison with these the *Apeiron* lacks concrete features, but this is why it constitutes an advance in understanding. Anaximander's step was crucial because he seems to have been the first to divest the symbol evoking the mystery of origin and destiny of all finite qualities derived from the finite features of items within experience. As Voegelin notes, it is still Anaximander's differentiated consciousness and the structure of its attendant symbolism which produce in this century Heidegger's careful distinction between Being and beings in the sense of things.[17]

When we talk of limitation in connection with the experience of finite existence in the infinite process of the real, we must remember its two aspects. By the term limitation we evoke not only the finitude of human existence, experience itself, in the transcending process, but also the limits of human knowledge of the whole. The infinite may be evoked symbolically but the totality is never known. This truth is forgotten in myth and in the Idealist systems of the nineteenth century. To see symbol as symbol, and not as description or fact, is the prime achievement of the differentiating symbols of theory — an achievement lost whenever the symbols of philosophy are misconstrued as achieved truths free from further trial by experience. By 'trial' I mean something wider than scientific testing. The truth of symbolism lies in its capacity to render experience intelligible, and the particular refinement of the symbols of philosophy is their power to clarify other, less differentiated levels of symbolic achievement. At neither the first nor the second level is experience definitively transcended. The role of philosophical concepts of the human sciences in relation to their object, the primary level of symbolic achievement, is to reflect the object so as to reveal how far the primary level falsifies the experience it articulates. In both cases experienced reality is the only valid point of reference.

The status and function of the symbols of philosophy must be considered if we are to understand the nature of ontology and the significance of such terms as 'essence' and 'nature' as the ontologist uses them. For these terms are indispensable to a realist conception of understanding and explanation in the sciences of man, and even those of nature. We experience reality as a process and know that our experience cannot be *all* of the real. Within the process, we experience the beings we encounter as particular types whose identifiable characteristics remain stable in time.

Thus we are bound to supplement the vocabulary of process with such terms as essence, nature or substance, which evoke that which persists in the process. These are the terms of persistence we refer to when we explain why a particular being behaved in a particular way, for in time we learn that mice or men tend to behave in certain ways under certain circumstances. When we say 'certain circumstances' we mean the relationship existing between the being whose behaviour we wish to explain and other beings manifesting identifiable natures. The nominalist view that such terms, which are universals describing all beings of a particular type, are nothing more than humanly devised labels seems to me to rest upon a confusion between the humanly created status of linguistic terms and the ontologically given character of the realities which they articulate. Thus the realist, anti-idealist view that consciousness is an ontological function of reality but not vice versa needs to be completed by a realist, anti-nominalist account of the status of universal as opposed to individual terms. We would not even begin to understand John Smith or his fellow men, unless each actualized to some degree the potentialities of man. Nor would the term 'fellow men' mean anything unless the individuals were fellow participants in a defining human nature. The Aristotelian language of act and potential and the Platonic notion of participation may not express perfectly what we are saying, but there are no terms that would do it better.

Let us consider the relationship between explanation and interpretative understanding in the light of this. The relationship is still the subject of considerable debate in the philosophy of social science — one where a considered realism can save us from needless confusion. Here, the primary task of the realist is to give an account of the interplay of understanding and explanation that operates in our scientific interpretation of the social world. This is a task of mediation and conciliation: the view that causal explanation and interpretative understanding are incompatible approaches to the same data is still widespread. First broached in the methodological debates of the late nineteenth century in Germany, the argument has been revived by English philosophers in the wake of the later writings of Wittgenstein. It would scarcely be an exaggeration to say that the debate that has raged since the publication of such books as Anscombe's *Intention* (1957) and Winch's *The Idea of a Social Science* has been between the two ghosts of Wittgenstein, the phantom of the logical positivist of the *Tractatus* and that of the linguistic philosopher of the *Philosophical Investigations*.

Anscombe and Winch both draw on Wittgenstein's later work in arguing against the reductivist tendencies of causal explanation in understanding human action. Anscombe uses Wittgenstein's theory of language games as discrete linguistic entities to argue that discussion of human action is couched in terms of a game irreducible to and untranslatable into the terms used in explaining natural events. Projects, motives, reasons and intentions, the staples of human action talk, are according to Anscombe elements of a language game separate from the vocabulary of cause, law, fact and explanation used in speaking of physical nature. The concept of cause, for instance, involves a confusion between incommensurate types of discourse when applied to the relationship between intention and achievement of a project, when, prompted by the vocabulary, we imagine that we mean the same thing as in the natural sciences.

Winch too is suspicious of the notion of cause when applied to human action. He argues that to understand such an action is to place it in its proper context of meaning and not to explain its generation in a causal manner. 'A man's social relations with his fellows', he declares, 'are permeated with his ideas about reality. Indeed, "permeated" is hardly a strong enough word: social relations are expressions of ideas about reality.'[18] Such arguments as these have contributed to a salutary reaction against the psychologically or physiologically reductive tendencies of positivism in social science, but they seem to isolate human phenomena from their natural baseline and divorce the procedures of the social and natural sciences. They give no account of the ontological conditions in which ideas arise and to which, the realist would claim, they creatively respond. In the terms of the older German debate, the realm of spirit is saved from the encroachments of naturalistic determinism but at the cost of de-materializing and de-ontologizing man as an agent in the world.

Anscombe's distinction between 'why' questions, which evoke the human order of motivation, and 'because of' questions, which refer to causality in the natural world, recalls Schutz's distinction between 'because' and 'in-order-to' motives. The former refer to the stimulus of past and present circumstances and the latter to consciously conceived projects. But while Anscombe assigns the two types of questions to separate realms of reality and discrete language games, Schutz sees the two as intelligibly related in our understanding of the social world.

In order to justify Schutz's conception of the relationship, we can begin by returning to Max Weber's definition of sociology:

> a science which attempts the interpretative understanding of social action in order thereby to arrive at a causal explanation of its course and effects. . . . Action is social in so far as, by virtue of the subjective meaning attached to it by the acting individual (individuals) it takes account of the behaviour of others, and is thereby oriented in its course.[19]

Weber suggests that interpretative understanding is the method the sociologist must follow to explain causally the course and effects of social action, which is, in turn, the basic unit of study for Weberian sociology. With the positivists, Weber seeks to establish sociology as a causal, explanatory science; with the historical idealists he insists upon interpretative understanding of the subjective meaning the actor attaches to the action as the means to achieve this.

The distinctiveness of this approach may be seen if we contrast it with Durkheim's view that the meaning the actor attaches to his act needs to be explained by reference to social facts external to and constraining upon the individual. Unlike Durkheim, Weber believes, first, that the actor's reasons for acting, seen in terms of his categories of meaning, are in reality the causes of his acting in a particular way; and, second, that the unit of the social action, defined as a conscious action oriented to the other, is the basic unit of sociological study. By implication, Durkheim's approach, treating subjective meanings as complex internalized effects of external and constraining causes is largely redundant, if we want to know why something happened rather than why it may have entered the prospective actor's field of consciousness.

The provisional ontological baseline of Weber's sociology — meaningful action — is different from Durkheim's — social facts. These are respectively the levels of unit of reality in terms of which each man's sociological explanations are cast. Of course Weber does not ignore the conditioning influence of surrounding circumstances. His historical studies make this clear. But he does reject the implication that 'conditioned' means 'determined' — a characteristic of Durkheim's approach. I call the ontological baseline provisional because, outside the theorist's own delineation of the scope of his inquiry, nothing stops the investigative mind from ranging further and deeper. The ontology of meaningful action and the ontology of social facts are themselves subjects of inquiry. An injunction, like that of Durkheim, to explain social facts in terms of other social facts, cannot forbid us the field. A provisional ontological baseline is justified in every science as a matter of economy, because unless such a level were fixed every investigation would expand into a cosmology and an ontology. However the division between disciplines is ultimately no firmer than the ontological isolation of the objects themselves and this, while sometimes valuable as a methodological procedure, is never true in reality.

From this perspective, which emphasizes the conventional and pragmatic status of interdisciplinary divisions and the unity of the real, Weber's approach seems more useful than Durkheim's even though it is Durkheim who investigates more deeply, striving to account for the social generation of meanings. Two reasons may be advanced for this. First, Weber avoids the social determinist implications of Durkheim's argument; and, second, he does not methodologically isolate social science from other levels and areas of inquiry. Nevertheless, Weber's treatment of his key terms, interpretative understanding and causal explanation, is theoretically unsatisfactory. Causality is assumed always to take the form that Aristotle called 'efficient causality.' This cuts out teleological, final causality, though it might be argued that this is no great loss since, at least within the limits of social science, something like it is readmitted through the attention paid to meaningful action and rational projects. More serious is the loss of any notion of either formal or material causality which, in the study of man, takes the form of explanations of human events as consequences of the sort of being who performs them and the sort of world in which they take place. The human sciences have been ill served by modern philosophers' rejection of Aristotle's theory of fourfold causality in favour of a single concept of efficient cause, and it is part of the realist's job to remedy this.

Weber's treatment of interpretative understanding is unsatisfactory too since he does not give a convincing account of how we identify the meaning which the act has for the actor. This problem is largely solved by Schutz in *The Phenomenology of the Social World*. Enough has been said about Schutz's critique of Weber to make further discussion redundant. However, in this context, Schutz's distinction between 'because' and 'in-order-to' motives has a useful part to play. 'In-order-to' motives are the crucial factors in explanations wherever an action is interpreted as the consequence of what the actor has it in mind to accomplish. We refer to 'because' motives, wherever the explanatory stress is placed upon surrounding and preceding circumstances which impinge upon the actor, whether he is conscious of them or not. When we ask why Mr X killed his aunt we may be asking either or both of two distinguishable questions. One can be answered in terms of his project of obtaining the money he believes to be left to him in her will. The other, the question of the 'because' motive, will refer to such factors as his previous relationship with his aunt and the influence exerted on him by keeping company with men willing to use violence to further their ends. This example of external influence reintroduces an element of the in-order-to type of explanation by referring to the furtherance of ends. This, like Schutz's use of 'motive' as a term covering both types, introduces an apparent confusion if we view the language of motivation and that of causality as belonging to discrete and incommensurate language games. But though two distinct questions coexist in the preposition 'why' when applied to human action, the distinction is only one between moments in the interpretation procedure *and* in the process of the action itself. In Ricoeur's words: 'Man is precisely the being who belongs at the same time to the regime of causality and to that of motivation, thus of explanation and of understanding.'[20] It is necessary both to distinguish the questions involved in understanding why an action took place and to remain aware of the ontological unity of the action which is being interrogated.

There are, Ricoeur notes, epistemological and ontological issues involved here:

On the epistemological level . . . there are not two methods, the explanatory method and the method of understanding. Strictly speaking, only explanation is methodic. Understanding is rather the non-methodic moment which, in the sciences of interpretation, comes together with the methodic moment of explanation. Understanding precedes, accompanies, closes and thus *envelops* explanation. In return, explanation develops understanding analytically.[21]

Explanation is the common goal of every science. To explain something in science is to say why it happened or why it is as it is: to give a causal account. Prior to this one must understand that an event has happened or that a being is present. This is the pre-scientific moment of understanding which the methodic, scientific explanation clarifies. Clarification, in its turn, deepens the understanding we have of the object. In particular, explanation furthers understanding by disclosing the patterns of causal dependence that operate in and on the object or event in question. In the human sciences, explanation depends upon the interpretative understanding of signs and symbols, each of which is an index of the creative involvement of a certain being in a certain world. Explanation, rooted most deeply in an ontological exploration of the constitutive features of man's being in the world, contributes to our understanding of the whole. From the perspective of realist ontology, causal explanation is regarded as the delineation of the patterns of dependence that bind reality in an identifiable order. Where, as in the human dimension, dependence is of a non-mechanistic sort, the model of causal explanation must admit the causal efficacy of conscious, rational agency. Man is such an agent, able to act upon the world within the limits of his nature and his context. To use the vocabulary of Aristotle, his action actualizes what is potential in nature but does not create out of nothing.

Epistemological issues open out into ontology. Reflection on the relationship of understanding to explanation in the human sciences leads us inevitably to a fundamental reflection on the ontological conditions of the dialectic in which they are joined.

If philosophy is concerned with 'understanding', [Ricoeur concludes] it is because it testifies, in the heart of epistemology, to a belonging of our being to the being which precedes every objectification, every opposition between subject and object. If the word *understanding* has such a density it is because, at the same time, it designates the non-methodic pole, dialectically opposed to the pole of explanation in every interpretative science, *and* it designates the indicator, no longer methodological but verifying, of the ontological relation of belonging of our being to beings and to Being. The rich ambiguity of the word *understanding* is that it designates a moment in the theory of method, the one we call the non-methodic pole, *and* the apprehension, at a level other than scientific, of our belonging to the whole of what is.[22]

8 Political Existence

Much of the impetus to the reorientation of the human sciences in recent years has come from the phenomenological movement. Each of the thinkers cited most frequently in the present book has significant links with the philosophical tendency associated, above all, with Edmund Husserl. It is useful at this point to consider these links, for the argument of *Realism*, while profoundly indebted to work carried out within the phenomenological tradition, aims, as its title tells, at recovering a perspective dismissed by Husserl himself as incurably naive and philosophically untenable since the work of Descartes.

The writings of Schutz have been the major vehicle for the introduction of Husserlian themes and concepts into sociology. On the evidence of *The Phenomenology of the Social World* Husserl described Schutz as: 'one of the few who have penetrated to the core of the meaning of my life's work'. It is notable that Schutz did not conceive his work in sociology as an extension of Husserl's transcendental phenomenology. Schutz's approach to social science is phenomenological because he directs the investigator away from the achieved forms of social order to the ways in which these forms come to be experienced as a world order in the life experience of the individual. In Schutz, as in Husserl, the motto is 'Back to the things themselves', and the 'things' to which we return from the flights of abstract speculation are phenomena, that is 'things' or objects as they appear to consciousness. But Schutz's phenomenological sociology is, as he described it, a constitutive phenomenology of the natural attitude, an account of the structures of the life-world of immediate experience. Such an account helps us recognize how our apprehension of the nature of things is a biographical process or, to use the terms of metaphysics, the manner in which we approach the order of being via the order of perception. Acceptance of this predisposes us neither to accept nor to reject Husserl's distinctive argument that the source of order must always lie in the activity of a transcendental subject. The phenomenology of the social world is a field of study complete in itself. Its justification is not to be found by reference to Husserl, though clues to its investigation will be. Rather, the work of Husserl is valuable because in social reality we truly

120

encounter a realm in which the subject, man the maker and victim of history, creates, within the limits set by the resistance of the real, a further level of objects. This level may loosely be called the world of culture. Because man is the source of culture, the course of human scientific studies leads us back to the genesis of cultural objects in the various encounters of man with the world into which he is born. Ambiguous though it may seem, Husserl's account of the constitution of the object in the experience of the subject, and the subsequent growth of the subject through contact with the constituted object, is, at the least, a revealing metaphor of the processes of social experience and cultural creation.

Voegelin's debt to Husserl is rather less clear than Schutz's. However the distinctive approach to the human sciences which Voegelin has developed in his work since the 1940s is centred in a philosophy of consciousness which, as we have seen, was formulated in reaction against Husserl's treatment of reality as a work of subjective constitution. To Husserl, Voegelin replies with an account of the exploratory workings of consciousness in history. It may seem odd that the reply to a philosophy of consciousness should take the forms of history and political science but Voegelin's point is precisely that a true philosophy of consciousness cannot do other than start with the field in which the work of consciousness is manifest. Following the example of Descartes, Husserl sought to achieve apodictic certainty. This for him was the distinguishing mark of a truly scientific philosophy. However, the price of such certainty is the abstraction of consciousness from the contingencies of existence and this, Voegelin implies, is unacceptable, for in existence alone is consciousness to be found. Beneath the differences of style and theme that divide Voegelin from Schutz is a common concern with the ways in which human consciousness achieves meaning in the world to which it is born and in which it is, in each individual case, an event. Schutz focuses on the micro or individual level, describing in detail the manner in which the individual comes to experience his environment as an ordered whole. Voegelin, on the macro or civilizational level, does the same thing, analysing the patterns of symbols through which men have made sense of their historical existence as part of a wider cosmic or temporal order. In the achievement of meaningful order, however precarious, men find the desired assurance that they are something other than absurdly pretentious side effects of the blind man's buff of physical forces. The work of Schutz and of Voegelin can be seen as a phenomenology of order, in that both are concerned to trace human accounts of order in reality to their roots in the life of consciousness. Phenomenologically considered, order is constituted out of the matter at hand, the intersubjectively given life-world for the individual in Schutz, the processes of history and cosmos for Voegelin. The shadow of irony in any such theory is that the claims of objective order are brought into question by an investigation that does not start out by making the assumption that meaning is a matter of discovery rather than creation. The term 'constitution' is sufficiently ambiguous to contain both possibilities.

Ricoeur is the French translator of Husserl and the author of several important essays on his philosophy. The turn to the hermeneutics of symbols in Ricoeur's work since *The Symbolism of Evil* is a result of problems encountered in the effort to achieve a directly reflective phenomenology of the will. Though Ricoeur's original project is thematically closer to the work of two other major influences, Marcel and Jaspers, his method owes more to the rigour of Husserl's phenomenological analysis. Eliade, too, is indebted to phenomenology. His attempt to describe the reality of religious experience and the meaning of religious symbols within the bounds of what Husserl called the *epoché* — the phenomenological reduction that allows us to grasp and articulate the essence of phenomena as they present themselves to consciousness without pronouncing judgement on their extramental reality — reveals this. Vivas, whose formulation of the nature of symbolic expression as simultaneously a work of creation and discovery is so pervasive an influence in the present work, was influenced in his break with the naturalism of John Dewey by the treatment of the objectivity of value which he found in the work of Max Scheler. Scheler ranks with Husserl himself among the founders of the phenomenological movement. All these men reject the reductionist approach which regards the human realm as a mere effect of the causal matrix of nature. Phenomenology, conceived broadly as 'an intuitive method for obtaining insights into essential structures'[1], opens the possibility of studying the world of consciousness and action without sacrificing the intellectual rigour which the methodologists of science rightly demand. As a method or mode of approach it retains its value even for those who do not accept Husserl's more ambitious claims.

It remains to answer the opening question of this inquiry: 'What is Social Reality?' The question demands an answer in terms of essential structures. It asks whether social science can identify a defining essence in social reality as experienced. To put it another way, what is the specific form of life which distinguishes human from other animal societies and is definitive of human community as such? The answer is that the social reality of man is essentially defined by the fact that human existence is political existence, and politics is a function of the creativity of man's response to the world. The quest for realism in social science leads, at so many points, to the renewal and strengthening of the links that bind sociology to philosophy, that it is not surprising if our inquiry leads back to Aristotle, the father of realist political philosophy. The path is different from his, and proceeds by detours through the work of later thinkers, but the core of human science remains what it was for Aristotle: a conception of man as a rational and political animal and of the *polis*, the formed community, as a work of reason accomplished in accord with the demands of human nature and within the limits set by the enveloping reality which the Greeks called *physis*.

Thus the links between sociology and philosophy relate the practice of sociological analysis to some of the most venerable as well as the most recent themes of philosophy. The question — what is social reality? — leads to a concern with ontology, the philosophical science of the universal characteristics of the real. This must be so, for the term reality, preceded by whatever adjective you choose, can only designate a level of being and never a separate and autonomous universe. To talk, as Schutz does, of multiple realities is to play upon a dangerous equivocation in language, though he is himself aware that each 'reality' — of dream of play or of fiction and so on — ontologically depends upon existence in the world disclosed to man. There are private perspectives but, strictly speaking, no private realities. Reality is what it is regardless of the play of the mind, and even a work of fiction which consciously departs from its universal defining characteristics, like many of those of Jorge Luis Borges, is dependent for its intelligibility upon the capacity, shared by author and reader, to recognize the modifications which the fantasist has carried out upon the fabric of the real. Fiction may be a vehicle of knowledge in that suspension of a constitutive element of reality in fantasy draws the reader's attention to something of which he is otherwise unaware. We seldom explicitly know best what we presume the most. That, incidentally, is why the findings of a phenomenology of the social world seem simultaneously so commonplace and so disorienting.

Another thread binding philosophy and the human sciences becomes clear when we ask how ontology is possible. For it is one thing to say that an ontology of social reality must be made explicit and quite another to say how it is to be done. There are three possibilities here. The first involves a completely naturalistic answer which identifies human nature with what physiology and biology tell us about the workings of the body, and which explains human works as complex effects of energy and matter conceived as the exclusive media of force in the universe. Such an approach reduces the rational, deliberative and creative functions of the mind to the physical responses of the body and therefore gives no account of the experiences of meaning, freedom and choice in human existence. Since these experiences are as much the stuff of life as the ever present consciousness of mortality, the naturalistic approach is inadequate. To say that meaning, freedom and choice are merely subjective delusions rooted in our relative ignorance of the web of causal necessity is no defence. The experience of significant choice cannot be shown to be delusory, nor can the naturalist successfully explain human creations as determined effects of ultimate physical causes. All attempts to do so have proved inadequate, as the history of determinist philosophies and behaviourist psychologies shows, and at the end the naturalist is left maintaining the quite unexceptionable but scarcely startling claim that physical circumstances give rise to problems and limit the range of possible responses in human life. This 'conclusion' is in fact merely the starting point for the real work of human science.

The other choices involve either a direct account of the essential structures of human existence in the world, in the manner of Heidegger's *Being and Time*, or an indirect approach, in the style of Ricoeur, who proceeds toward ontology through the interpretation of the symbols in which men articulate their experience of existence. To choose the latter course does not imply a denigration of the former. There is much of value in Heidegger's analysis of *Dasein*, man's being-there in the world, or, to use Sartre's phrase without espousing its Sartrian meaning, the human condition. The temporal structure of existence, the awareness of looming oblivion, the projective nature of action, and the practical rather than purely cognitive style of our everyday participation in the world are indeed universal constituents of life of which the sociologist must remain aware. But it is the universality of Heidegger's *Dasein* analysis which limits its value as a model for the ontology of social reality. For in social reality the essentials of existence are not all there is to know. By taking the indirect path through the interpretation of symbols we can account for the variety of human response to life — an area left largely unexamined in the more direct approach of Heidegger's early writings.

The human sciences must proceed to the discovery of the fundamental contours of human existence by analysing the symbolic expressions which embody, in all their historical and individual specificity, the results of man's creative reaction to being in the world. It is possible to distinguish different modes of response, each of which is a particular manifestation of what Vivas calls the basic symbolic activity. Vivas himself distinguishes four distinct modes: the aesthetic, the cognitive, the religious and the moral. However, as he admits, 'to reduce the heterogeneous and diversified activities of man in culture . . . to only four distinct modes is to make full use of the well-nigh unlimited coefficient of elasticity of words, and this is particularly the case as regards the term *moral,* which, if the classification is to be exhaustive, must be used to include all practical activity.'[2] The particular names we attach to the different modes are, of course, less significant than our recognition that each is a specific application of a fundamental human capacity which facilitates the embodiment of the meaning of the real in humanly created forms. The result of such application, the cultural work or social institution, is always more than a reflection of its equivalent experience. The symbol serves up reality in digestible form and simultaneously points beyond the immediacy of brute experience to the wider context in which each object of experience is placed in intelligible order. Symbols point to the ultimate mysteries of transcendence but leave no question of relationship unanswered.

Even a figurative painting, apparently the most simply imitative of symbolic achievements, is always more than a copy of a natural reality.

Before the spectator it activates awareness of more than, as an imitation, it would seem to contain. A painting embodies an articulation of a certain aspect of man's life in the world, a point brought out supremely well in Heidegger's celebrated analysis of Van Gogh's depiction of the shoes of a peasant woman:

> From the dark opening of the worn insides of the shoes the toilsome tread of the worker stares forth. In the stiffly rugged heaviness of the shoes there is the accumulated tenacity of her slow trudge through the far-spreading and ever-uniform furrows of the field swept by a raw wind. On the leather lie the dampness and richness of the soil. Under the soles slides the loneliness of the field-path as evening falls. In the shoes vibrates the silent call of the earth, its quiet gift of the ripening grain and its unexplained self-refusal in the fallow desolation of the wintry field. This equipment is pervaded by uncomplaining worry as to the certainty of bread, the wordless joy of having once more withstood want, the trembling before the impending childbed and shivering at the surrounding menace of death.[3]

Jonas defined understanding as an experience of shared potential, mediated by symbols. We bring our own human experience to the task of following Heidegger's analysis, but the creative work of the artist evokes an element of self-awareness which is the reverse of private. In crucial ways the facts of life that define the world evoked by Van Gogh's painting, that set its limits, form its hopes and fears, are our defining realities as well, or, at the least, might be. Failure to see this is a failure in self-knowledge, a pathological myopia of the anthropological imagination, the essence of sympathy, communication and understanding. The peasant shoes, a creation of Van Gogh, symbolize experienced truth discovered in the life of the species, a truth about that life and its context. The case is, if anything, even clearer in a literary work, where the form of fiction focuses the mind of the reader or audience on an actual or potential truth about the world of fact. Nor do we find anything different in the field of interpretative sociology, where the actualized forms of institutions are comprehensible because they more or less successfully embody certain human possibilities which are universal.

In his discussions of ontology, Nicolai Hartmann distinguishes between two modes of Being, the real and the ideal. The real, which includes everything that occupies a place in space and time, is further divided into strata of reality which correspond to the levels of inorganic nature, organic nature, consciousness and superindividual culture. The levels of consciousness and culture are the bearers of ideals, universals such as values and numbers, which depend for their existence upon these two higher levels of reality. The levels of real Being are hierarchically related in that the existence of the higher presupposes the existence of the lower. There is no culture where there is not consciousness, no consciousness without organic nature, and so forth. At each step the emergence of the higher level is marked by its partial independence from the laws that govern the lower. Thus consciousness achieves a relative autonomy from organic nature, and culture a certain freedom from consciousness. It is the understanding of the partial but real freedom of cultural achievement which constitutes the field of a philosophical social science. Ontological awareness is a matter of taking account of the pattern of dependence which underlies the level of culture and limits the scope of its autonomy.

This may be expressed in simple common-sense terms. We take for granted that there are certain features of the physical universe which are absolutely necessary for survival, for instance, a broad constancy in the amount of heat received from the sun and the proportion of oxygen in the atmosphere we breathe. These are aspects of the natural baseline which permits but does not determine the higher yet dependent level of human action. Action is never carried out in isolation from surrounding reality. Each conscious individual acts each day. He makes decisions which are significant for him because the consequences will, however minutely, be different for him according to his choice and will alter his chances of realizing his projects. This is what is presupposed in the notion of man as a free being — this and no more. Freedom cannot mean total and unconditioned autonomy of the individual actor, for such an autonomy could only be the lot of a disembodied decision-making apparatus — one that had contact neither with any similar being nor with the resistance to action characteristic of every item of inorganic and organic nature. Freedom is a feature of the human capacity to come to considered decisions in the context of a natural and social environment which, to a considerable degree, exercises constraining influence upon their content and result. Content and result must be distinguished: the phenomenon of the unintended consequence always divides the intention from the achievement of action. Even the mental processes which are the vehicle of conscious choice are not ours to choose but are aspects of our nature as human beings. In the terms of Hartmann's ontology, they belong to the stratum of organic nature more than to that of consciousness. We may choose what we think but we do not choose how. Such limitations are not an alienation of human freedom but its constitutive form.

Social reality is brought into existence by the activity of the species man in the world. Superindividual culture, the intersubjectively available life-world into which each child is born, embodies the sense-endowing achievements of consciousness. While consciousness is always individual consciousness (there is no such thing as a group mind), culture is super-individual. The cultural level attains a partial independence from consciousness because it embodies the achieved acts of consciousness. The obvious example is that of language. The concepts of language originate in individual moments of consciousness. Someone at some time first spoke the word which articulated the concept of a dog. He did this in order to speak of a significant item in his experience, as, many millennia later, a less anonymous figure was to speak of 'oxygen'. The articulation of a concept in a word fixes it as an element of language, a shared cultural reality whose meaning is learned but not decided by the consciousness of the individual. I am not speaking of the structure of language — which may, as Chomsky believes, be quasi-genetically determined — but of its cognitive content, the items of experience which are intelligibly linked for each in the fabric of a mother tongue. The shared reality of culture is what we mean when, suggestively but not altogether accurately, we speak with Durkheim of a "conscience collective". A cultural reality exists independently of any individual consciousness.

To understand social reality is to see the way in which it belongs to the pre-existing enveloping reality of the universe. From earlier arguments it is clear that its belonging consists in a dependence out of which it emerges as a relatively free level of Being. The creative nature of human works, the ability of the artist to make novel objects that correspond to nothing beyond themselves, or the power of social conventions to mould the individual's experience of reality, can lead one to forget the limits of this independence. Such works seem to attain a freedom from all outside circumstances which they do not truly possess. This happens when the work of art is treated as a pure manifestation of the expressive drive of the artist, or the network of socially accepted definitions is treated as actually constitutive of reality. In fact the creative use of symbols, whether in works of art or social institutions, is always a response to the tension of existence in a world created neither by the individual nor the species. Thus the most apparently autonomous creations of man remain potentially so many indices of human participation in a reality whose order invites exploration. Cultural creations articulate insights and discoveries which man makes about the world. Because of their symbolic form, we do not see them as direct answers to unequivocal questions but as modes of action or expression found to be appropriate to the case. It is, nevertheless, as answers to still available questions that they are most readily understood.

It remains to examine the specific symbolic function of political institutions in the context of the philosophy of symbol — a philosophy that takes the establishment of meaning as central to symbolic activity. We must, in the first place, recognize that the symbolic dimension is something wider than the presence of conscious symbols in the life of an institution. The symbols which men treasure apparently irrationally, chains and robes of office, trade union or national banners, titles such as King or Comrade, are genuine in that they stand for and evoke an aspect of social existence which could not be appropriately expressed in another way. The fact that one man addresses another as 'Your Majesty' or as 'Comrade' tells us something about the self-understanding and actual life of the cultures in which the terms are spoken. The fact, attested so ironically this century, that the Comrade may wield greater power than the King shows merely that the order of symbols is no mere reflection of the order of power but embodies a legitimating self interpretation of the political order. Terms like 'King' or 'Comrade' signify that a certain person has a particular place in the conceptual scheme by which society makes sense of its existence or, justifies itself to itself and to others. One of the most interesting political phenomena of recent decades has been the way in which the spread of egalitarian symbols has served to legitimate the creation of new systems of factually unequal power relations. When men called Louis XIV 'King' they articulated a truth about the political position of the man who bore the title: while 'Comrade' Stalin expressed only the legitimating lie which pretended that Soviet society had moved beyond the ancient order of power and subservience. This is something we see repeating itself wherever egalitarian ideologies take root.

Institutions themselves serve as symbols too, in that they represent and habitualize modes of action which are, in origin, creative responses to the tensions of life in the world. It is easy to understand the popularity which the Marxist buys by arguing that there is nothing final about the political order and that institutions alienate man from what he might otherwise be. In considering abstractly what we might be, consciousness wanders freely beyond the limitations that concretely make us what we are. Where the Marxist interpretation falls down is not only in its economistic view of the foundation of political order but at the limit that any hermeneutics of suspicion must reach. A system of thought which limits itself to interpreting the forms of political life as fundamentally alienating must necessarily fail to grasp the extent to which these forms are the very condition of human survival.

This amounts to a misunderstanding of the political existence which is the essence of social reality. Man's being a political animal explains the distinctive nature of human society. Man shares sociality with other creatures as well, no doubt, as certain genetically inherited patterns of orientation to his fellows and the environment, but as a political animal he is, so far as we know, unique. What this means is that in his case the constitutionally given social need for coexistence with his fellows is not satisfied by a biologically determined pattern of instinctive response. The need for society is naturally given but the achieved forms of human sociality are, as the Thomists put it, works of reason. The programmed patterns of response to which ethologists like Konrad Lorenz and Robert Ardrey have drawn our attention are no more than the limiting framework for the genuine novelty achieved in historical existence. That is why Aristotle described man as a being both rational and political. A rational being is not a being who always acts reasonably but one with the capacity to reason: he is able to come to decisions after conscious processes of deliberation. These take the form of individual deliberation, the estimation of possibilities by the self, and the social form of debate. These are the processes involved in the formation and survival of the institutions of political life.

Emphasis on processes of consciousness does not imply the view that the source of political society lies in a conscious decision or series of decisions. Deliberation and debate, the rational, political alternative to the instinct of lower animals, are subsequent to sociality, whose forms they specify within the limits of the possible. The source of society, the ontological ground of social reality, is the nature of man and of the universe in which he participates. Only the specific forms of participation are unfixed: about participation and its conditions there is no choice. We do not cease to be part of reality by pretending that we are not. Nor do we alter the real possibilities of our existence by thinking them to be other than they are. At the same time we must acknowledge the apparently opposed view that, in Peter Winch's words: 'social relations are expressions of ideas about reality'.[4] The tension between realist and idealist accounts of social reality must be resolved in an ontology which admits the effective reality of the relatively independent realm of ideas, while not forgetting the essential dependence of the thought upon the thinker and the thinker upon the world. This is done when, like Hartmann, we understand the structure of real and ideal Being to be a hierarchy of dependence and emergence, in which the real freedom achieved by the higher level never negates its dependence upon the lower. The only exception to this dependence of the higher upon the lower is found in the field of cosmogony where, at the limit, we pose the question of the origin of the cosmos itself. Voegelin's theory of symbolism allows us to redescribe what Winch calls 'ideas about reality' in terms that do not contradict our fundamental realism. Ideas about reality are symbols through which men make intelligible and communicable the experience of participation in a process which is ontologically non-dependent upon the human participant. Realist sociology sees the institutional structure of society as a human creation, rationally and politically formed more than naturally determined, which arises and develops through a series of more or less appropriate responses to the discovered features of being in the world. Political society is the articulation of a rational being for action in the world.

Finally, the political order mediates between the individual and the cosmic processes which govern the natural and the social worlds. The form of mediation varies according to how men make sense of the transcendent reality of infinite time and space. In the empires of the ancient Near East the New Year ceremonies, in which the king played the central role, provided an occasion for the affirmation of an identity between the order of society and the cosmic order — an identity apprehended in the pattern of returning seasons and the regular movement of the stars. If we understand the high gods of the empire as the symbolic embodiment of the suprahuman forces which govern the ultimate order of the universe, we see at once that such rites affirm the meaning of life by integrating the order of social reality with an enveloping order which shows apparent permanence and regularity. Where the archaic conception of cyclical or reversible time is eclipsed by the characteristically modern view that time is unidirectional and irreversible, where the myth of eternal recurrence is replaced in consciousness by the arrow of time, it becomes the function of the political order to mediate between man and the course of history. By way of example, consider the Soviet leaders standing on the dais before the Lenin mausoleum each May Day. The power of these men rests in their control over the coercive apparatus of the Soviet state, but their authority is rooted in a philosophy of history according to which the world proletariat are the chosen people of history and the Soviet Communist Party is the organized vanguard of their movement. Ideologically the institutions of Soviet Russia mediate between man and a course of historical events of which, without the ideology, no ultimate sense could be made. In the face of unendurable silence society makes its claim to be the vehicle of meaning, the ways of participation in the mysterious yet not impenetrable destiny to which we are born. A society that fails in this will inspire neither devotion from within nor respect from without. It stands in spite of its secular virtues, on the edge of oblivion.

Notes

Chapter 1 What is Social Reality?

1 Eric Voegelin, *The New Science of Politics* (University of Chicago Press 1952), p. 4.
2 pp. 4-5.
3 Alfred Schutz, *Collected Papers*, edited and with introduction by Maurice Natanson, 3 vols. (The Hague: Martinus Nijhoff 1962-6), 1, pp. 58-9.
4 Voegelin, p. 29.
5 Schutz, 1, p. 306.
6 p. 312.
7 p. 329.
8 p. 330.
9 pp. 330-31.
10 p. 293.
11 p. 297.
12 Mircea Eliade, *Images and Symbols*, translated by Philip Mairet (London: Harvill Press 1961), p. 12.
13 Schutz, 3, pp. 83-4.
14 Marvin Farber, op. cit. (New York: Harper 1966), p. 47.
15 Schutz, 1, p. 149.
16 p. 332.
17 p. 335.
18 Eliseo Vivas, *Creation and Discovery: essays in criticism and aesthetics* (New York: Noonday 1955), p. 123.
19 Maurice Natanson, ed., *Phenomenology and Social Reality* (The Hague: Martinus Nijhoff 1970).
20 Alfred Schutz, *The Phenomenology of the Social World* (London: Heinemann Educational 1972), p. 241.

Chapter 2 The Foundation of Interpretative Sociology

1 This is not to ignore the extent to which Kant's problem is itself rooted in the subjectivism prevalent in Western philosophy after Descartes.

2 Anthony Giddens, *Durkheim* (London: Harvester and Fontana 1978).
3 Hans Jonas, 'Change and Permanence: on the possibility of under-standing history' in *Social Research*, 38, 3 (Autumn 1971), pp. 498-528.
4 p. 498.
5 p. 500.
6 p. 502.
7 Etienne Gilson, *L'Etre et l'Essence* (Paris: Vrin 1972), p. 362.
8 Jonas, pp. 505-6.
9 p. 507.
10 pp. 510-11
11 pp. 517-18
12 p. 525.
13 Paul Ricoeur, *The Symbolism of Evil*, translated by Emerson Buchanan (New York: Harper & Row 1967).
14 Peter Winch, *The Idea of a Social Science and its Relation to Philosophy* (London: Routledge & Kegan Paul 1958), p. 87.
15 Paul Filmer et al, *New Directions in Sociological Theory* (London: Collier-Macmillan 1972).
16 In *W. Dilthey, Selected Writings*, edited and translated by H. P. Rickman (Cambridge University Press 1976).
17 In Anthony Giddens, ed. *Positivism and Sociology* (London: Heinemann 1974). p. 28.
18 Eric Voegelin, *Order and History*, 4 vols, vol 5 forthcoming (Louisiana State University Press 1955-74).
19 Gregor Sebba, 'Order and Disorders of the Soul: Eric Voegelin's Philosophy of History', *Southern Review* (1967), p. 287.

Chapter 3   On Interpretation

1 Mircea Eliade, *No Souvenirs: journal 1967-1969*, translated by Fred H. Johnson, jr (New York: Harper & Row 1973; London: Routledge & Kegan Paul 1978), pp. 289-90.
2 Voegelin, *The New Science of Politics*, p. 27.
3 Paul Ricoeur, 'The Model of the Text', *Social Research* 38, 3 (Autumn 1971) pp. 529-62.
4 Paul Ricoeur, *The Conflict of Interpretations: Essays in hermeneutics*, ed. Don Ihde (North Western University 1974), p. 16.
5 pp. 65-6.
6 See note 3 above.
7 *W. Dilthey, Selected Writings*, p. 249.
8 p. 262.
9 ibid.
10 Ricoeur, 'The Model of the Text', pp. 557-8.
11 p. 537.

12 p. 540.
13 p. 541.
14 pp. 542-3.
15 pp. 543-4.
16 pp. 544-5.

Chapter 4   Symbol, Myth and Theory

 1 Eric Voegelin, *Anamnesis,* translated and edited by Gerhart Niemeyer
    (University of Notre Dame 1978), pp. 21-2.
 2 Paul Ricoeur, *The Symbolism of Evil,* p. 5.
 3 Voegelin, p. 33.
 4 Eric Voegelin, 'Equivalences of Experiences and Symbolization in
    History', in *Eterniz e Storia* (Florence: 1970), p. 228.
 5 Eric Voegelin, *Order and History 1 Israel and Revelation,* p. 2.
 6 Peter Berger, *Facing up to Modernity* (London Basic Books 1972) p.
    204.
 7 Don Ihde, *Hermeneutic Phenomenology: the philosophy of Paul
    Ricoeur* (North Western University Press 1971).
 8 Mircea Eliade, *Patterns in Comparative Religion,* translated by
    Rosemary Sheed (London and New York: Sheed & Ward 1958).
 9 Peter Berger and Thomas Luckmann, *The Social Construction of
    Reality* (London: Basic Books 1972) p. 204.
10 p. 79.
11 p. 110.
12 p. 112.
13 p. 113.
14 pp. 121-2.
15 This is a major theme of *Israel and Revelation* (note 5 above).
16 George Steiner, *In Bluebeard's Castle: some notes on the redefinition
    of culture* (London: Faber 1971), p. 106.

Chapter 5   The Edge of Suspicion

 1 Mircea Eliade, 'Methodological Remarks on the Study of Religious
    Symbolism' in M. Eliade and Joseph M. Kitawaga, eds., *The History of
    Religions: essays in methodology* (University of Chicago Press 1959),
    pp. 88-9.
 2 See chapter 2.
 3 Rudolph Carnap, 'Overcoming Metaphysics' in Michael Murray, ed.,
    Heidegger and Modern Philosophy: critical essays (Yale University
    Press 1978), pp. 32-3.
 4 p. 30.

5 Karl R. Popper, *The Logic of Scientific Discovery* (London: Hutchinson.

6 William A. Earle, *Objectivity: an essay in phenomenological ontology* (Chicago: Quadrangle Books, revised edition 1968).

7 Charles E. Reagan and David Stewart, eds., in *The Philosophy of Paul Ricoeur: an anthology of his work* (Boston: Beacon 1978), p. 188.

8 Cited by Theodore Wiesengrund-Adorno in *Negative Dialectics* (London: Routledge & Kegan Paul 1973), p. 128.

9 Earle, p. 93.

10 See Ricoeur, *The Conflict of Interpretations* and *Freud and Philosophy* (Yale University Press 1970).

11 Adorno, pp. 121-2.

12 Ricoeur, *Freud and Philosophy*, p. 46.

13 ibid.

14 Adorno, p. 65.

Chapter 6   The Call from Beyond

1 Theodore Wiesengrund-Adorno, *Negative Dialectics*, p. 3.

2 Karl Marx and Frederick Engels, *Selected Works* (London: Lawrence & Wishart 1968), p. 620.

3 Georg Lukács, *Toward the Ontology of Social Being: Marx* (London: Pluto Press 1978), pp. 71-2.

4 Karl Marx. *Early Writings,* introduction by Lucio Colletti (London: New Left Books and Penguin 1975), p. 44.

5 Marx and Engels, p. 182.

6 Thomas Molnar, *God and the Knowledge of Reality* (New York: Basic Books 1973), p. 150.

7 Jacob Loewenberg, ed., *Hegel: Selections* (New York: Scribners 1929), p. 16.

8 Herbert Marcuse, *Reason and Revolution: Hegel and the rise of social theory,* 2nd edition (London: Routledge & Kegan Paul 1955), pp. 44-6.

9 ibid.

10 Marcuse, p. 165.

11 Voegelin, *Anamnesis*, p. 76.

12 Alasdair C. MacIntyre, *Marcuse:* (London: Collins 1970), p. 16.

13 Herbert Marcuse, *Negations,* translated by Jeremy J. Shapiro (London: Allen Lane 1968), p. 43.

14 pp. 45-6.

15 p. 57.

16 p. 56.

17 p. 54.

18 p. 65.

19 pp. 66-7.

20 Alfred Schmidt, *The Concept of Nature in Marx* (London: New Left Books 1971), p. 162.

21 p. 121.

22 p. 122.

23 Cited by Ernest Bloch, *A Philosophy of the Future*, translated by John Cumming (New York: Herder 1970), pp. 19-20.

24 Max Horkheimer, *Critical Theory: selected essays*, translated by J. O'Connell and others (New York: Herder 1972), pp. 53-4.

25 pp. 59-60.

26 pp. 258-9.

27 Theodore Wiesengrund-Adorno, *Prisms*, translated by S. and S. Weber (London: Neville Spearman 1967), pp. 31-2.

28 Max Horkheimer, *Eclipse of Reason* (New York- Oxford University Press 1947), p. 93.

29 p. 94.

30 p. 176.

31 p. vi.

32 Max Horkheimer, 'Schopenhauer today' in K. H. Wolff et al, eds, *The Critical Spirit: essays in honour of Herbert Marcuse* (Boston: Beacon 1967), p. 70.

33 Adorno, *Negative Dialectics*, p. 320.

34 p. 321.

35 p. 21.

36 p. 25.

37 pp. 355-6.

38 Martin Jay, *The Dialectical Imagination: a history of the Frankfurt School and the Institute of Social Research 1923-1950* (London: Heinemann Educational 1973), p. 57.

39 Horkheimer, *Critical Theory*, p. 17.

40 pp. 19-21.

41 pp. 198-9.

42 p. 24.

43 Adorno, *Negative Dialectics*, p. 141.

44 Horkheimer, *Eclipse of Reason*, pp. 181-2.

45 Etienne Gilson, *L'Etre et l'Essence*.

46 Jacques Maritain *The Degrees of Knowledge* (London: Bles 1937).

47 Jacques Maritain, *Three Reformers: Luther, Descartes, Rousseau* (London: Sheed & Ward 1928).

48 Jay, p. 46.

49 p. 279.

50 Horkheimer, *Critical Theory*, p. viii.

51 p. ix.

52 Adorno, *Negative Dialectics*, pp. 362-3.

53 Ernest Bloch, *Man on his Own: essays on the philosophy of religion*, translated by E. B. Ashton (New York: Herder 1970), p. 23.

Chapter 7   Aspects of Realism

1 Martin Heidegger, *Basic Writings from 'Being and Time' (1927) to 'The Task of Thinking' (1964)* edited and with introduction by David Farrell Krell (London: Routledge & Kegan Paul 1978), p. 214.
2 Albert Camus, *The Rebel* translated by Anthony Bower (Hamish Hamilton 1953).
3 Eric Voegelin, *Anamnesis*, p. 4.
4 p. 11.
5 p. 12.
6 Eric Voegelin, 'Equivalences of Experiences and Symbolization in History' in *Eterniz e Storia*, p. 223.
7 In Maurice Natanson, ed., *Phenomenology and Social Reality*.
8 pp. 186-7.
9 *'Poetry and Abstract Thought'* in *Paul Valéry: an anthology*, selected and with introduction by James Lawler (London: Routledge & Kegan Paul 1977), p. 142.
10 Voegelin, *Anamnesis*, p. 33.
11 p. 75.
12 ibid.
13 Charles E. Reagan and David Stewart, eds., *The Philosophy of Paul Ricoeur*, p. 150.
15 Schutz, *Collected Papers*, 1, p. 329.
16 Voegelin, *Anamnesis*, pp. 26-7.
17 Voegelin, *Order and History*, 4, *The Ecumenic Age*, pp. 175-6.
18 Peter Winch, *The Idea of a Social Science and its Relation to Philosophy*, p. 23.
19 Max Weber, *The Theory of Social and Economic Organization* (Glencoe: Free Press 1957), p. 1.
20 Reagan and Stewart, eds., p. 158.
21 p. 165.
22 pp. 165-6.

Chapter 8   Political Existence

1 Herbert Spiegelberg, *The Phenomenological Movement: a historical introduction*, 2 vols, (The Hague: Martinus Nijhoff 1960), 1, p. 11.
2 Eliseo Vivas, *The Artistic Transaction and Essays on the Theory of Literature* (Ohio State University Press 1963), pp. 11-12.
3 Martin Heidegger, 'The Origins of the Work of Art', in *Basic Writings*. p. 163.
4 Peter Winch, *The Idea of a Social Science*, p. 23.

Index